Latin Phrases

MW01128186

VERITAS
VOS LIBERABIT

"The Truth Will Set You Free!"

Introduction

Have you ever wondered what "Quid pro quo" means? - *Something for something, i.e. a favor for a favor.* How about "Non sequitur"? - *It does not follow.* Now, right at your very fingertips, we have assembled the most complete compendium of Latin phrases for your convenience. Everything is arranged in alphabetical order....so enjoy and dazzle the world with your intelligence and writing power.

A

A bene placito - *At one's pleasure*
A capite ad calcem - *From head to heel*
A cappella - *In church [style] - i.e. Vocal music only*
A contrario - *From a contrary position*
A cruce salus - *From the cross comes salvation*
A Deo et Rege - *From God and the King*
A fortiori - *With yet stronger reason*
A fronte praecipitium a tergo lupi - *A precipice in front, wolves behind (between a rock and a hard place)*
A mari usque ad mare - *From sea to sea (Motto of Canada)*
A mensa et thoro - *From board and bed (legal separation)*
A pedibus usque ad caput - *From feet to head*
A posse ad esse - *From possibility to actuality*
A posteriori - *From what comes after. Inductive reasoning based on observation, as opposed to deductive, or a priori*
A priori - *From what comes before*
A verbis ad verbera - *From words to blows*
Ab absurdo - *From the absurd (establishing the validity of your argument by pointing out the absurdity of your opponent's position)*
Ab aeterno - *From the beginning of time*
Ab asino lanam - *Wool from an ass, blood from a stone impossible*
Ab hinc - *From here on*
Ab imo pectore - *From the bottom of the chest. (from the heart) (Julius Caesar)*
Ab incunabulis - *From the cradle*
Ab initio - *From the beginning*

Ab intestato - *Having made no will*

Ab origine - *From the origin*

Ab ovo usque ad mala - *From the egg right to the apples (From start to finish) (*Horace*)*

Ab ovo - *From the egg*

Ab urbe condita - *From the foundation of the city. (Rome)*

Ab/Ex uno disce omnes - *From one person, learn all people*

Abiit, excessit, evasit, erupit - *He has left, absconded, escaped and disappeared*

Absente reo - *In absence of the defendant*

Absit invidia - *No offence intended*

Absit omen - *May the omen be absent. (may this not be an omen)*

Absum! - *I'm outta here!*

Abusus non tollit usum - *Wrong use does not preclude proper use*

Abutebaris modo subjunctivo denuo - *You've been misusing the subjunctive again*

Abyssus abyssum invocat - *Hell calls hell; one mistep leads to another*

Accipere quam facere praestat injuriam - *It is better to suffer an injustice than to do an injustice*

Acta est fabula, plaudite! - *The play is over, applaud! (Said to have been emperor Augustus' last words)*

Acta non verba - *Action not words*

Acta sanctorum - *Deeds of the saints*

Actus reus - *Wrongful act - as opposed to mens rea - the wrongful intention or guilty mind*

Ad absurdum - *To the point of absurdity*

Ad acta - *To archives. Not actual any more*

Ad alta - *To the summit*

Ad astra per aspera - *To the stars through difficulty*

Ad astra - *To the stars*

Ad augusta per angusta - *To high places by narrow roads*

Ad captandum vulgus - *To appeal to the crowd -- often used of politicians who make false or insincere promises appealing to popular interest*

Ad clerum - *To the clergy*

Ad eundem gradum - *To the same level*

Ad eundem - *Of admission to the same degree at a different university*

Ad eundum quo nemo ante iit - *To boldly go where no man has gone before*

Ad fontes - *To the sources (motto of Renaissance Humanism)*

Ad fundum - *To the bottom / To the end (said during a generic toast, like bottoms up!)*

Ad hoc - *For a particular purpose. (improvised, made up in an instant)*

Ad hominem - *Appealing to a person's physical and emotional urges, rather than her or his intellect*

Ad honorem - *In honour. Honour not baring any material advantage*

Ad idem - *Of the same mind*

Ad infinitum - *To infinity without end*

Ad interim - *For the meantime*

Ad libitum (Acronym 'ad lib') - *At one's pleasure*

Ad Libitur - *As Desired*

Ad limina apostolorum - *To the thresholds of the Apostles*

Ad litem - *For a lawsuit or action*

Ad locum - *At the place*

Ad lucem - *Towards the light (motto of the University of Lisbon)*

Ad maiorem dei gloriam (AMDG) - *For the greater glory of God*

Ad multos annos - *To many years!, i.e. Many happy returns!*

Ad nauseum - *To the point of making one sick*

Ad perpetuam rei memoriam - *For the perpetual remembrance of the thing*

Ad praesens ova cras pullis sunt meliora - *Eggs today are better than chickens tomorrow (a bird in the hand is worth two in the bush)*

Ad referendum - *Subject to reference*

Ad rem - *To the point*

Ad valorem - *By the value, e.g. Ad valorem tax*

Ad vitam aeternam - *For all time*

Ad vitam paramus - *We are preparing for life*

Ad vitam - *For life*

Addendum - *A thing to be added*

Adeste Fideles - *Be present, faithful ones*

Adsum - *Here! present!*

Adversus incendia excubias nocturnas vigilesque commentus est - *Against the dangers of fires, he (Augustus) conceived of the idea of night guards and watchmen*

Adversus solem ne loquitor - *Don't speak against the sun (don't waste your time arguing the obvious)*

Advocatus diaboli - *The devil's advocate*

Aegrescit mcdendo - *The disease worsens with the treatment. The remedy is worse than the disease*

Aegri somnia - *A sick man's dreams (Horace)*

Aegroto, dum anima est, spes esse dicitur - *It is*

said that for a sick man, there is hope as long as there is life

Aequam memento rebus in arduis servare mentem - *Remember when life's path is steep to keep your mind even. (Horace)*

Aeronavis abstractio a prestituto cursu - *Hijacking*

Aetatis (aet.) - *Age*

Aeternum vale - *Farewell forever*

Affidavit - *A sworn written statement usable as evidence in court*

Age quod agis - *Do what you do well, pay attention to what you are doing*

Age. Fac ut gaudeam - *Go ahead. Make my day!*

Agenda - *Things to be done*

Agnus Dei - *The Lamb of God*

Aio, quantitas magna frumentorum est - *Yes, that is a very large amount of corn*

Alea iacta est - *The die has been cast. (Caesar)*

Alias - *Otherwise*

Alibi - *Elsewhere*

Aliena nobis, nostra plus aliis placent - *Other people's things are more pleasing to us, and ours to other people. (Publilius Syrus)*

Alis volat propiis - *She flies with her own wings (state motto of Oregon)*

Alma Mater - *Nourishing mother. (One's old school or university)*

Alter ego - *Other 'I' or 'Other Self'*

Alter ipse amicus - *A friend is another self*

Alterum ictum faciam - *I'm going to take a mulligan*

Altissima quaeque flumina minimo sono labi - *The deepest rivers flow with the least sound. (still* *waters run deep)*

Alumnus - *Nursling (former pupil)*

Amantes sunt amentes - *Lovers are lunatics*

Amantium irae amoris integratio est - *The quarrels of lovers are the renewal of love. (Terence)*

Amare et sapere vix deo conceditur - *Even a god finds it hard to love and be wise at the same time*

Amat victoria curam - *Victory favors those who take pains*

Amicitiae nostrae memoriam spero sempiternam fore - *I hope that the memory of our friendship will be everlasting. (Cicero)*

Amicule, deliciae, num is sum qui mentiar tibi? - *Baby, sweetheart, would I lie to you?*

Amicus certus in re incerta cernitur - *A true friend is discerned during an uncertain matter*

Amicus curiae - *Friend of the court*

Amicus humani generis - *A friend of the human race (philanthropist)*

Amicus verus est rara avis - *A true friend is a rare bird*

Amor animi arbitrio sumitur, non ponitur - *We choose to love, we do not choose to cease loving. (Syrus)*

Amor caecus est - *Love is blind*

Amor est vitae essentia - *Love is the essence of life. (Robert B. Mackay)*

Amor ordinem nescit - *Love does not know order. (St. Jerome)*

Amor patriae - *Love of country*

Amor platonicus - *Platonic love*

Amor tussisque non celantur - *Love, and a cough, are not concealed. (Ovid)*

Amor vincit omnia - *Love conquers all. (Virgil)*

Amoto quaeramus seria ludo - *Joking aside, let us turn to serious matters. (Horace)*

An nescis, mi fili, quantilla sapientia mundus regatur? - *Don't you know then, my son, how little wisdom rules the world?*

Anguis in herba - *A snake in the grass. A treacherous person. (Vergil)*

Anicularum lucubrationes - *Old wives' tales*

Animadvertistine, ubicumque stes, fumum recta in faciem ferri? - *(At a barbeque) Ever noticed how wherever you stand, the smoke goes right into your face?*

Animis opibusque parati - *Prepared in minds and resources (ready for anything)*

Animus facit nobilem - *The spirit makes (human) noble*

Anno (an.) - *Year*

Anno domini (AD) - *In the year of the Lord*

Anno hegirae (AH) - *In the year of the hegira*

Anno mundi - *In the year of the world*

Anno regni - *In the year of reign*

Anno urbis conditae (AUC) - *From the year of founding of the city (Rome)*

Annuit coeptis - *God has favored us*

Annus bisextus - *Leap year*

Annus horribilis - *A horrible year*

Annus mirabilis - *Year of wonders*

Ante litteram - *Before the letter*

Ante meridiem (a.m.) - *Before midday*

Ante mortem - *Before death*

Ante prandium (A.p.) - *Before a meal*

Ante - *Before*

Antebellum - *Before the war*

Antiquis temporibus, nati tibi similes in rupibus ventosissimis exponebantur ad necem - *In the good old days, children like you were left to perish on windswept crags*

Anulos qui animum ostendunt omnes gestemus! - *Let's all wear mood rings!*

Apage Satanas - *Begone, Satan*

Appareo Decet Nihil Munditia? - *Is It Not Nifty?*

Apudne te vel me? - *Your place or mine?*

Aqua fortis - *Nitric acid*

Aqua pura - *Pure water*

Aqua vitae - *Water of life (brandy)*

Aquila non captat muscas - *The eagle doesn't capture flies (don't sweat the small things)*

Arbiter elegantiae - *Judge in matters of taste*

Arcana imperii - *Secrets of the empire*

Arduum sane munus - *A truly arduous task*

Arguendo - *For the sake of argument*

Argumentum ad hominem - *An argument against the man. Directing an argument against an opponent's character rather than the subject at hand*

Argumentum ad ignorantiam - *Arguing from ignorance*

Armis Exposcere Pacem - *They demanded peace by force of arms. (An inscription seen on medals)*

Ars gratia artis - *Art for art's sake. (motto of MGM)*

Ars longa, vita brevis - *Art (work) is long, but life is short*

Ars sine scienta nihil est - *Art without science is nothing. (I would also claim that the opposite is true)*

Artium baccalaureus - *Bachelor of Arts (BA)*

Artium magister - *Master of Arts (MA)*

Ascendo tuum - *Up yours*

Asinus asinum fricat - *The ass rubs the ass. (Conceited people flatter each other about qualities they do not possess)*

Aspice, officio fungeris sine spe honoris amplioris - *Face it, you're stuck in a dead end job*

Aspirat primo Fortuna labori - *Fortune smiles upon our first effort. (Virgil)*

Assiduus usus uni rei deditus et ingenium et artem saepe vincit - *Constant practice devoted to one subject often outdues both intelligence and skill. (Cicero)*

Astra inclinant, non necessitant - *The stars incline; they do not determine*

Astra non mentiuntur, sed astrologi bene mentiuntur de astris - *The stars never lie, but the astrologs lie about the stars*

Aude sapere - *Dare to know*

Audaces fortuna iuvat - *Fortune favors the bold. (Virgil)*

Audere est facere - *To dare is to do. (Motto of Tottenham Hotspur)*

Audi et alteram partem - *Hear the other side too*

Audiatur et altera pars! - *Let us hear the opposite side!*

Audio, video, disco - *I hear, I see, I learn*

Auget largiendo - *He increases by giving liberally*

Aura popularis - *The popular breeze. (Cicero)*

Aurea mediocritas - *The golden mean. (an ethical goal; truth and goodness are generally to be found in the middle.) (Horace)*

Auribus tenere lupum - *I hold a wolf by the ears. (I am in a dangerous situation and dare not let go.)*

(Terence)
Aurora australis - *The Southern lights*
Aurora borealis - *The Northern lights*
Aurora Musis amica - *Dawn is friend of the muses. (Early bird catches the worm.)*
Aut Caesar aut nihil - *Caesar or nothing i.e., all or nothing*
Aut disce aut discede - *Either learn or leave*
Aut insanit homo, aut versus facit - *The fellow is either mad or he is composing verses. (Horace)*
Aut viam inveniam aut faciam - *I will either find a way or make one*
Aut vincere aut mori - *Either conquer or die*
Auxilio ab alto - *By help from on high*
Avarus animus nullo satiatur lucro - *A greedy mind is satisfied with no (amount of) gain*
Ave atque vale - *Hail and farewell. (Catullus)*
Ave caesar! Morituri te salutamus - *Hail Caesar! We who are about to die salute you. (gladiators before the fight)*
Ave maria - *Hail Mary*

B

Balaenae nobis conservandae sunt! - *Save the whales!*
Beata Virgo (Maria) - *The Blessed Virgin (Mary)*
Beatae memoriae - *Of blessed memory*
Beati pacifici - *Blessed are the peacemakers*
Beati pauperes spiritu - *Blessed are the poor in spirit*
Beati possidentes - *The happy who possess. (possession is nine points of the law) (Euripides)*
Beatus - *The blessed one*
Bella detesta matribus - *Wars, the horror of*

mothers. (Horace)

Bella gerant alii - *Let others wage war*

Bellum omium contra omnes - *Everyman's struggle against everyman. (Thomas Hobbes)*

Belua multorum es capitum - *The people are a many-headed beast*

Bene legere saecla vincere - *To read well is to master the ages. (Professor Isaac Flagg)*

Bene qui latuit, bene vixit - *One who lives well, lives unnoticed. (Ovid)*

Bene, cum Latine nescias, nolo manus meas in te maculare - *Well, if you don't understand plain Latin, I'm not going to dirty my hands on you*

Bene - *Good*

Beneficium accipere libertatem est vendere - *To accept a favour is to sell freedom. (Publilius Syrus)*

Bibere venenum in auro - *Drink poison from a cup of gold*

Bis dat qui cito dat - *He gives twice who quickly gives. (Publius Syrus)*

Bis in die (bid) - *Twice a day*

Bis interimitur qui suis armis perit - *He is doubly destroyed who perishes by his own arms. (Syrus)*

Bis repetita placent - *The things that please are those that are asked for again and again. (Horace)*

Bis vincit qui se vincit in victoria - *He conquers twice who in the hour of conquest conquers himself. (Syrus)*

Bis vivit qui bene vivit - *He lives twice who lives well*

Bona fide - *In good faith. i. e. well-intentioned, fairly*

Bona fides (noun) - *Honest intention*

Bona fortuna - *Good luck!*

Bona officia - *Good services's*
Bonum commune communitatis - *General welfare. Literally, common good of the community*
Bonum commune hominis - *Common good of man*
Bonum vinum laetificat cor hominis - *Good wine gladdens a person's heart*
Bovina Sancta! - *Holy cow!*
Braccae illae virides cum subucula rosea et tunica Caledonia-quam elenganter concinnatur! - *Those green pants go so well with that pink shirt and the plaid jacket!*
Braccae tuae aperiuntur - *Your fly is open*
Brevior saltare cum deformibus mulieribus est vita - *Life is too short to dance with ugly women*
Brevior saltare cum deformibus viris est vita - *Life is too short to dance with ugly men*
Brevis esse latoro obscurus fio - *When I try to be brief, I speak gobbledegook*
Brevis ipsa vita est sed malis fit longior - *Our life is short but is made longer by misfortunes. (Publilius Syrus)*
Busillis - *Baffling puzzle or difficult point*

C

Cacoethes scribendi - *An insatiable urge to write. (Juvenal)*
Cadit quaestio - *The question drops*
Caeca invidia est - *Envy is blind. (Livy)*
Caeci caecos ducentes - *Blind are led by the blind. Leaders are not more knowledgeable than the ones they lead*
Caeli enarrant gloriam Dei - *The heavens declare the glory of God*

Caelum non animum mutant qui trans mare currunt - *They change the sky, not their soul, who run across the sea. (Horace)*

Caelum videre iussit, et erectos ad sidera tollere vultus - *He bid them look at the sky and lift their faces to the stars. (Ovid)*

Caesar si viveret, ad remum dareris - *If Caesar were alive, you'd be chained to an oar*

Camera obscvra - *Hidden room - an early photographic or painting technique utilizing optical pinholes*

Canis meus id comedit - *My dog ate it*

Canis timidus vehementius latrat quam mordet - *A timid dog barks more violently than it bites. (Curtius Rufus)*

Capillamentum? Haudquaquam conieci esse! - *A wig? I never would have guessed!*

Caro putridas es! - *You're dead meat*

Carpe Cerevisi - *Seize the beer!*

Carpe diem, quam minimum credula postero - *Seize the day, trust as little as possible in tomorrow. (Horace)*

Carpe diem - *Seize the day. (opportunity) (Horace)*

Casus belli - *An act used to justify war*

Catapultam habeo. Nisi pecuniam omnem mihi dabis, ad caput tuum saxum immane mittam - *I have a catapult. Give me all your money, or I will fling an enormous rock at your head*

Casus belli - *Event (that is the justification for, or the cause) of war*

Causarum justia et misericordia - *For the causes of justice and mercy*

Causa mortis - *Death Cause*

Cave ab homine unius libri - *Beware of anyone who has just one book. (Latin Epigram)*

Cave canem, te necet lingendo - *Beware of the dog, he may lick you to death*

Cave canem - *Beware of the dog*

Cave cibum, valde malus est - *Beware the food, it is very bad*

Cave ne ante ullas catapultas ambules - *If I were you, I wouldn't walk in front of any catapults*

Cave quid dicis, quando, et cui - *Beware what you say, when, and to whom*

Cave - *Beware!*

Caveat emptor - *Let the buyer beware. (He buys at his own risk)*

Caveat venditor - *Let the seller beware*

Caveat - *Let him/her beware*

Cedant arma togae - *Let arms yield to the toga. (Let violence give place to law)*

Cedo maiori - *I yield to a greater person*

Certamen bikini-suicidus-disci mox coepit? - *Does the Bikini-Suicide-Frisbee match start soon?*

Certe, toto, sentio nos in kansate non iam adesse - *You know, Toto, I have a feeling we're not in Kansas anymore*

Certum est, quia impossibile - *It is certain, because it is impossible. (Tertullianus)*

Cetera desunt - *The rest is missing*

Ceteris paribus - *All else being equal*

Christus rex - *Christ the King*

Cineri gloria sera venit - *Fame comes too late to the dead*

Circa (c.) - *Approximately*

Clamo, clamatis, omnes clamamus pro glace

lactis - *I scream, you scream, we all scream for ice cream*

Clara pacta, boni amici - *Clear agreements, good friends*

Codex Juris Canonici - *Book of canon law*

Cogita ante salis - *Think before you leap, or look before you leap*

Cogitationis poenam nemo patitur - *Nobody should be punished for his thoughts*

Cogito ergo doleo - *I think therefore I am depressed*

Cogito sumere potum alterum - *I think I'll have another drink*

Cogito, ergo sum - *I think, therefore I am. (Reni Descartes)*

Commodum ex iniuria sua nemo habere debet - *No person ought to have advantage from his own wrong*

Commune bonum - *The common good*

Commune periculum concordiam parit - *Common danger brings forth harmony*

Communi consilio - *By common consent*

Compos mentis - *Of sound mind (and judgement)*

Concordia discors - *Discordant harmony*

Concordia res parvae crescent - *Work together to accomplish more*

Conditio sine qua non - *Condition without which not, or an essential condition or requirement*

Confer (cf.) - *Compare*

Confiteor - *I confess*

Congregatio de Propaganda Fide - *Congregation for the Propagation of the Faith*

Coniecturalem artem esse medicinam - *Medicine*

is the art of guessing. (Aulus Cornelius Celsus)

Coniunctis viribus - *With united powers*

Conlige suspectos semper habitos - *Round up the usual suspects*

Consensu omnium - *By the agreement of all*

Consensus audacium - *An agreement of rash men. (a conspiracy) (Cicero)*

Consuetudinis magna vis est - *The force of habit is great. (Cicero)*

Consule planco - *In the consulship of Plancus (In the good old days) (Horace)*

Consummatum est - *It is completed (Christ's last words, John 19:30)*

Contra felicem vix deus vires habet - *Against a lucky man a god scarcely has power*

Contra mundum - *Against the world*

Contraria contrariis curantur - *The opposite is cured with the opposite. (Hippocrates)*

Coram populo - *In the presence of the people. (Horace)*

Cornix cornici oculos non effodiet - *A crow doesn't rip out the eyes of another crow*

Cornucopia - *Horn of plenty*

Corpus christi - *The body of Christ*

Corpus delicti - *The body of a crime. (The substance or fundamental facts of a crime)*

Corpus Juris Canonici - *The body of canon law*

Corpus Juris Civilis - *The body of civil law*

Corpus vile - *Worthless body*

Corrigenda - *A list of things to be corrected. (in a book)*

Corripe Cervisiam - *Seize the beer!*

Corruptio optimi pessima - *Corruption of the best*

is worst

Coruscantes disci per convexa caeli volantes - *Flying saucers*

Cotidiana vilescunt - *Familiarity breeds contempt*

Cotidie damnatur qui semper timet - *The man who is constantly in fear is every day condemned. (Syrus)*

Crapulam terriblem habeo - *I have a terrible hangover*

Cras amet qui nunquam amavit; Quique amavit, cras amet - *May he love tomorrow who has never loved before*

Credidi me felem vidisse! - *I tought I taw a puddy tat!*

Credite amori vera dicenti - *Believe love speaking the truth. (St. Jerome)*

Credo elvem etiam vivere - *I believe Elvis lives*

Credo nos in fluctu eodem esse - *I think we're on the same wavelength*

Credo quia absurdum - *I believe it because it is absurd. (contrary to reason) (Tertullian)*

Credo ut intelligam - *I believe in order that I may understand. (St. Augustine)*

Credula vitam spes fovet et melius cras fore semper dicit - *Credulous hope supports our life, and always says that tomorrow will be better. (Tibullus)*

Crescit amor nummi, quantum ipsa pecunia crevit - *The love of wealth grows as the wealth itself grew. (Juvenalis)*

Crescite et multiplicamini - *Increase and multiply*

Crimen falsi - *Perjury*

Crudelius est quam mori semper timere mortem

- It is more cruel to always fear death than to die. (Seneca)

Crux - *Puzzle*

Cui bono? - *For whose benefit is it? (a maxim sometimes used in the detection of crime) (Cicero)*

Cui dono lepidum novum libellum? - *To whom do I give my new elegant little book? (Catullus)*

Cui malo? - *Who suffers a detriment?*

Cui peccare licet peccat minus - *One who is allowed to sin, sins less. (Ovid)*

Cuius regio, eius religio - *He who rules, his religion*

Cuiusvis hominis est errare; nullius nisi insipientis in errore perseverare - *Any man can make a mistake; only a fool keeps making the same one*

Cuivis dolori remedium est patientia - *Patience is the cure for all suffer*

Culpa - *A sin*

Culpam poena premit comes - *Punishment closely follows crime as its companion. (Horace)*

Cum catapultae proscriptae erunt tum soli proscript catapultas habebunt - *When catapults are outlawed, only outlaws will have catapults*

Cum grano salis - *With a grain of salt. (Pliny the Elder?)*

Cum homine de cane debeo congredi - *Excuse me. I've got to see a man about a dog*

Cum laude magnum - *With great success*

Cum laude - *With praise*

Cum tacent, clamant - *When they remain silent, they cry out. (Their silence speaks louder than words) (Cicero)*

Cum - *With*

Cur etiam hic es - *Why are you still here?*

Cura nihil aliud nisi ut valeas - *Pay attention to nothing except that you do well. (Cicero)*

Cura posterior - *A later concern*

Cura ut valeas - *Take care*

Curae leves loquuntur ingentes stupent - *Slight griefs talk, great ones are speechless. (minor losses can be talked away, profound ones strike us dumb)*

Curriculum vitae - *The course of one's life*

Cursum perficio - *My journey is over, or I finish my journey*

Custos morum - *Guardian of morals*

D

Da mihi basilia mille - Kiss me with a thousand kisses

Da mihi castitatem et continentiam, sed noli modo! - Make me chaste and pure, but not yet!

Da mihi sis bubulae frustrum assae, solana tuberosa in modo gallico fricta, ac quassum lactatum coagulatum crassum - Give me a hamburger, french fries, and a thick shake

Da mihi sis cerevisiam dilutam - I'll have a light beer

Da mihi sis crustum Etruscum cum omnibus in eo - I'll have a pizza with everything on it

Damnant quod non intellegunt - They condemn what they do not understand

Data et accepta - Expenditure and receipts

De asini vmbra disceptare - To argue about the shadow of an ass. (petty things for petty mind)

De bene esse - It shall be so, as long as it is well

De die in diem - From day to day

De duobus malis, minus est semper eligendum - Of two evils, the lesser must always be chosen (Thomas a Kempis)

De facto - Something that is automatically accepted

De gustibus non est disputandum - There's no accounting for taste

De inimico non loquaris sed cogites - Don't wish ill for your enemy; plan it

De integro - Repeat again from the start

De iure - By law. According to law

De minimis non curat praetor - The authority or king, or law does not care about trivial things

De minimis - With respect to trifles

De mortuis nil nisi bonum - Say nothing but good about the dead. (Chilon)

De nihilo nihil - Nothing comes from nothing. (Lucretius)

De novo - Anew

De profundis - Up from the depths (of misery)

De rervm natvra - On the nature of things. (title of Marcus Aurelius's magnum opus)

Decrevi - I have decreed

Dei gratia - By the grace of God

Delenda est carthago - Carthage must be destroyed

Dente lupus, cornu taurus petit - The wolf attacks with his fang, the bull with his horn. (Horace)

Deo adiuvante - With God's help

Deo favente - With God's favour

Deo gratias - [We give] thanks to God

Deo Optimo Maximo - To God, the Best, the Greatest

Deo vindice - God will prove us right. (motto of the

Confederate States of America)

Deo volente - God willing

Desunt cetera - The rest is missing

Deus absconditus - A god who is hidden from man

Deus commodo muto consisto quem meus canis sententia existo - Which, in a very ham-fisted way, with generosity, comes close to being

Deus et natua non faciunt frusta - God and nature do not work together in vain

Deus ex machina - A contrived or artificial solution. (literally, 'a god from a machine')

Deus Misereatur - May God Have Mercy

Deus vobiscum - God be with you

Deus volent - (as) God will

Deus vult! - God wills it! (Slogan of the Crusades)

Di! Ecce hora! Uxor mea me necabit! - God, look at the time! My wife will kill me!

Diabolus fecit, ut id facerem! - The devil made me do it!

Dic mihi solum facta, domina - Just the facts, ma'am

Dictum sapienti sat est - A word to a wise person is sufficient

Die dulci freure - Have a nice day

Diem perdidi - I have lost a day (another day wasted) (Titus)

Dies felices - Happy Days

Dies Irae - Day of Wrath, or Judgment Day

Dies natalis - Birthday

Dies non - Business free day

Difficile est longum subito deponere amorem - It is difficult to suddenly give up a long love. (Catullus)

Difficile est saturam non scribere - It is hard not

to write satire. (Juvenalis)

Difficile est tenere quae acceperis nisi exerceas - It is difficult to retain what you may have learned unless you should practice it. (Pliny the Younger)

Diis aliter visum - The Gods decided otherwise

Diligentia maximum etiam mediocris ingeni subsidium - Diligence is a very great help even to a mediocre intelligence. (Seneca)

Diligite justitiam, o judices terrae - Cherish justice, o judges of the earth

Dimidium facti qui coepit habet - Half is done when the beginning is done. (Horace)

Dira necessitas - The dire necessity. (Horace)

Discere docendo - To learn through teaching

Disiecti membra poetae - Limbs of a dismembered poet. (Horace)

Disjecta membra - The scattered remains

Divide et impera - Divide and conquer

Dixi - I have spoken. (I will say no more on the matter, and no one else may speak further)

Do ut des - I give so that you give back

Docendo discitur - It is learned by teaching. (Seneca)

Doli capax - Capable of crime

Domine, dirige nos - Lord, direct us

Domino optimo maximo - To the Lord, the best and greatest

Dominus illuminatio mea - The Lord is my light

Dominus providebit - The Lord will provide

Dominus tecum - May the Lord be with you (Singular)

Dominus vobiscum - May the Lord be with you (Plural)

Domus dulcis domus - Home sweet home

Donec eris felix, multos numerabis amicos - As long as you are fortunate, you will have many friends (when you are successful, everyone wants to be your friend)

Donna nobis pacem - Grant us peace

Draco dormiens nunquam titillandus - Never Tickle a Sleeping Dragon. (motto of Harry Potter's alma mater)

Dramatis personae - Characters of the play

Duc, sequere, aut de via decede - Lead, follow, or get out of the way

Ducator meus nihil agit sine lagunculae leynidae accedunt - My calculator does not work without batteries

Duco ergo sum - I calculate therefore I am

Dulce bellum inexpertis - War is sweet for those who haven't experienced it. (Pindaros)

Dulce est desipere in loco - It is sweet to relax at the proper time

Dulce et decorum est pro patria mori - It is sweet and glorious to die for one's country. (Horace)

Dulcius ex asperis - Through difficulty, sweetness

Dum excusare credis, accusas - When you believe you are excusing yourself, you are accusing yourself. (St. Jerome)

Dum inter homines sumus, colamus humanitatem - As long as we are among humans, let us be humane. (Seneca)

Dum spiramus tuebimur - While we breathe, we shall defend

Dum spiro, spero - While I breathe, I hope. (Cicero)

Dum tempus habemus, operemur bonum - While we have the time, let us do good

Dum vita est spes est - While life is, hope is. / While there is life there is hope

Dum vivimus, vivamus - While we live, let us live (Epicurean)

Dura lex, sed lex - The law is harsh, but it is the law

E

E contrario - *From a contrary position*

E pluribus unum - *From many, one (motto of the USA)*

E re nata - *As circumstances dictate*

E vestigio - *From where one stands*

Ecce homo - *Behold the man*

Ecce signum - *Behold the proof*

Editio princeps - *First printed edition*

Ego et rex meus - *I and my King*

Ego me bene habeo - *With me all is well. (last words) (Burrus)*

Ego nolo caesar esse - *I don't want to be Caesar. (Florus)*

Ego spem pretio non emo - *I do not purchase hope for a price. (I do not buy a pig in a poke.)*

Ego - *Consciousness of one's own identity*

Eheu fugaces labuntur anni - *Alas, the fleeting years slip by. (Horace)*

Eheu, litteras istas reperire non possum - *Unfortunately, I can't find those particular documents*

Eiusdem generis - *Of the same kind*

Elizabeth Regina/Eduardus Rex (E.R.) - *Queen Elizabeth/King Edward*

Emeritus - *Honorary; by merit*

Emitte lucem et veritatem - *Send out light and truth*

Ense et aratro - *With sword and plow. (citizen-soldier, one who serves in war and peace)*

Eo ipso - *By that very act*

Eo nomine - *Under that name*

Epistula non erubescit - *A letter doesn't blush. (Cicero)*

Eram quod es, eris quod sum - *I was what you are, you will be what I am. (grave inscription)*

Ergo bibamus - *Therefore, let us drink*

Ergo - *Therefore*

Errare humanum est - *To err is human. / It is human to err. (Seneca)*

Errata - *A list of errors (in a book)*

Erratum (errata) - *Error (errors)*

Escariorium lavator - *Dishwashing machine*

Esse est percipi - *Being is perception. (It is a standard metaphysical) (Mauser)*

Esse quam videri - *To be, rather than to seem (state motto of North Carolina)*

Est autem fides credere quod nondum vides; cuius fidei merces est videre quod credis - *Faith is to believe what you do not see; the reward of this faith is to see what you believe. (St. Augustine)*

Est deus in nobis - *The is a god inside us*

Est modus in rebus - *There is a middle ground in things. (Horace)*

Est queadam fiere voluptas - *There is a certain pleasure in weeping. (Ovid)*

Estne tibi forte magna feles fulva et planissima? - *Do you by chance happen to own a large,* *yellowish, very flat cat?*

Estne volumen in toga, an solum tibi libet me videre? - *Is that a scroll in your toga, or are you just happy to see me?*

Esto perpetua - *Let it be forever*

Esto perpetue - *May you last for ever*

Et alii/aliae - *Other persons/things*

Et cetera/etcetera (etc.) - *And the rest*

Et in arcadia ego - *I, also, am in Arcadia*

Et sequens (et seq.) - *And the following*

Et sequentes (et seq. Or seqq.) - *And those that follow*

Et sic de ceteris - *And so to of the rest*

Et tu, Brute - *And you, Brutus*

Et uxor (abbreviated et ux.) - *And wife*

Etiam capillus unus habet umbram - *Even one hair has a shadow. (Publilius Syrus)*

Eventus stultorum magister - *Events are the teacher of the stupid persons. Stupid people learn by experience, bright people calculate what to do*

Ex abrupto - *Without preparation*

Ex abundancia cordis, os loquitor - *From the abundance of the heart the mouth speaks*

Ex animo - *From the heart (sincerely)*

Ex ante - *Before the event, beforehand. (economics: based on prior assumptions)*

Ex cathedra - *From the chair. With authority (without argumentation)*

Ex cearulo - *Out of the blue*

Ex curia - *Out of court*

Ex dolo - *Intentionally*

Ex gratia - *Purely as a favour*

Ex hypothesi - *From the hypothesis. (i.e. The one*

under consideration)

Ex libris - *From the Library (of)*

Ex luna, scientia - *From the moon, knowledge. (motto of Apollo 13)*

Ex mea sententia - *In my opinion*

Ex more - *According to custom*

Ex nilhilo nihil fit - *Nothing comes from nothing*

Ex officio - *By virtue of his office*

Ex opere operato - *By the work having been worked*

Ex parte - *By only one party to a dispute in the absence of the other*

Ex post facto - *After the fact, or Retrospectively*

Ex proprio motu - *Voluntarily*

Ex silentio - *From silence. (from lack of contrary evidence)*

Ex tempore - *Off the cuff, without preparation*

Ex uno disce omnes - *From one person learn all persons. (From one we can judge the rest)*

Ex vi termini - *By definition*

Ex voto - *According to one's vow*

Ex - *Out of*

Excelsior - *Ever upward. (state motto of New York)*

Exceptio probat regulam de rebus non exceptis - *An exception establishes the rule as to things not excepted*

Exceptis excipiendis - *Excepting what is to be excepted*

Excitabat fluctus in simpulo - *He was stirring up billows in a ladle. (He was raising a tempest in a teapot) (Cicero)*

Excusatio non petita, accusatio manifesta - *He who excuses himself, accuses himself (qui* *s'excuse, s'accuse)*

Exeat - *Permission for a temporary absence*

Exegi monumentum aere perennius - *I have erected a monument more lasting than bronze. (Horace)*

Exempli gratia (e.g) - *For the sake of example*

Exeunt omnes - *All go out. (A common stage direction in plays)*

Exeunt - *They go out*

Exit - *He/she goes out*

Exitus acta probat - *The outcome proves the deeds. (the end justifies the means) (Ovid)*

Experientia docet stultos - *Experience teaches fools*

Experientia docet - *Experience is the best teacher*

Experimentum crucis - *Critical experiment*

Expressio unius est exclusio alterius - *The mention of one thing may exclude others*

Extempore - *Without premeditation*

Exterioris pagina puella - *Cover Girl*

Extinctus amabitur idem - *The same [hated] man will be loved after he's dead. How quickly we forget. (Horace)*

Extra ecclesiam nulla salus - *Outside the Church [there is] No Salvation. (A phrase of much disputed significance in Roman Catholic theology)*

Extra territorium jus dicenti impune non paretur - *The judgment (or the authority) of one who is excceding his territorial jurisdiction is disobeyed with impunity*

F

Fabas indulcet fames - *Hunger sweetens the beans, or hunger makes everything taste good!*

Faber est suae quisque fortunae - *Every man is the artisan of his own fortune. (Appius Claudius Caecus)*

Faber quisque fortunae suae - *Each man (is) the maker of his own fortune*

Fabricati diem - *Make my day*

Fac me cocleario vomere! - *Gag me with a spoon!*

Fac ut nemo me vocet - *Hold my calls*

Fac ut vivas - *Get a life*

Facile princeps - *Acknowledged leader*

Facilis descensvs averno - *The descent to Avernus (Hell) it's easy to fall, hard to rise*

Facilius est multa facere quam diu - *It is easier to do many things than to do one for a long time. (Quintilianus)*

Facilius per partes in cognitionem totius adducimur - *We are more easily led part by part to an understanding of the whole. (Seneca)*

Facito aliquid operis, ut te semper diabolus inveniat occupatum - *Always do something, so that the devil always finds you occupied. (St. Jerome)*

Facta, non verba - *Deeds, not words. (Actions speak louder than words)*

Factum est - *It is done*

Fallaces sunt rerum species - *The appearances of things are deceptive. (Seneca)*

Falsus in uno, falsus in omnibus - *False in one thing, false in all*

Fama crescit eundo - *The rumour grows as it goes. (Vergil)*

Fama nihil est celerius - *Nothing is swifter than rumor*

Fama semper vivat - *May his/her fame last forever*

Fama volat - *The rumour has wings. (Vergil)*

Fames est optimus coquus - *Hunger is the best cook*

Farrago fatigans! - *Thuffering thuccotash!*

Fas est et ab hoste doceri - *It's proper to learn even from an enemy. (Ovid)*

Favete linguis - *To keep a (religious) silence. (Horace)*

Fax mentis incedium gloriae - *The passion of glory is the torch of the mind*

Fecit (fec.) - *Made by*

Feles mala! cur cista non uteris? stramentum novum in ea posui - *Bad kitty! Why don't you use the cat box? I put new litter in it*

Feles mala! - *Bad kitty!*

Felis qvi nihil debet - *Happy [is] he who owes nothing*

Felix culpa - *Happy fault*

Felix qui potuit rerum cognoscere causas - *Happy is he who has been able to learn the causes of things. (Vergil)*

Felo de se - *Suicide*

Fere libenter homines id quod volunt credunt - *Men readily believe what they want to believe. (Caesar)*

Festina lente - *Make haste slowly*

Fiat justitia (et ruat caelum) - *Let justice be done. (though the heavens fall)"*

Fiat lux - *Let there be light*

Fiat volvntas tua - *Let Thy will [be done] (Biblical)*

Fiat - *Let it be done*

Fide, non armis - *By faith, not arms*

Fidei defensor - *Defender of the faith*
Fides punica - *Treachery. (Livy)*
Fides quaerens intellectum - *Faith seeking understanding*
Fidus Achates - *Faithful Achates (friend)*
Filioque - *And from the son*
Filius nullius - *A bastard*
Finem respice - *Look to the end [before setting forth]*
Finis coronat opus - *The ending crowns the work. (Ovid)*
Finis - *The end*
Flagrante delicto - *Literally while the crime is blazing. Caught red-handed, in the very act of a crime*
Flamma fumo est proxima - *Flame follows smoke. (there is no smoke without fire) (Plautus)*
Floreat regina regina - *May it flourish. (motto of the City of Regina, Saskatchewan Canada)*
Floruit - *Flourished*
Fluctuat nec mergitur - *It is tossed by the waves but it does not sink*
Fons et origo - *The source and origin*
Forsan et haec olim meminisse iuvabit - *Perhaps someday we will look back upon these things with joy*
Forsan miseros meliora sequentur - *For those in misery perhaps better things will follow. (Virgil)*
Fortes et liber - *Strong and free. (Alberta)*
Fortes fortuna adiuvat - *Fortune favors the brave. (Terence)*
Fortes fortuna iuvat - *Fortune favours the brave*
Fortiter fideliter forsan feliciter - *Bravely,*

faithfully, perhaps successfully

Fortiter in re, suaviter in modo - *Resolutely in action, gently in manner. (To do unhesitatingly what must be done but accomplishing it as inoffensively as possible)*

Fortitudine vincimus - *By endurance we conquer*

Fortius quo fidelius - *Strength through loyalty*

Fortuna amicos parat, inopia amicos probat - *The fortune is preparing friends, the abundance is testing them*

Fortuna vitrea est; tum cum splendet frangitur - *Fortune is glass; just when it gleams brightest it shatters*

Fortuna caeca est - *Fortune is blind. (Cicero)*

Fortunatus sum! Pila mea de gramine horrido modo in pratum lene recta volvit! - *Isn't that lucky! My ball just rolled out of the rough and onto the fairway!*

Frangar non flectar - *I am broken, I am not deflected*

Frater, ave atque vale - *Brother, hello and good-bye. (Catullus)*

Fronti nulla fides - *No reliance can be placed on appearance. (don't judge a book by its cover)*

Frustra laborant quotquot se calculationibus fatigant pro inventione quadraturae circuli - *Futile is the labor of those who fatigue themselves with calculations to square the circle. (Michael Stifel, 1544)*

Fugit hora - *The hour flies*

Fugit inreparabile tempus - *Irretrievable time flies. (Virgil)*

Functus officio - *Having discharged his duty and*

thus ceased to have any authority over a matter
Furnulum pani nolo - *I don't want a toaster*

G

Gaudeamus igitur (iuvenes dum sumus) -
Therefore, let us rejoice. (while we are young)
Genius loci - *The guardian spirit of the place*
Gens togata - *The toga-clad race; the romans*
Genus irritabile vatum - *The irritable race of poets.
(Horace)*
Gladiator in arena consilium capit - *The gladiator
is formulating his plan in the arena (i.e., too late)
(Seneca)*
Gloria filiorum patres - *The glory of sons is their
fathers*
Gloria in excelsis deo - *Glory to God in the highest*
Gloria Patri - *Glory to the Father*
Gloria virtutis umbra - *Glory (is) the shadow of
virtue*
Gloria - *Glory*
Gloriosum est iniurias oblivisci - *It is glorious to
forget the injustice*
Gnothe seauton (Greek) - *Know thyself*
Graeca sunt, non leguntur - *It is Greek, you don't
read that*
Gramen artificiosum odi - *I hate Astroturf*
Gratia placenti - *For the sake of pleasing*
Graecia capta ferum victorem cepit - *Captive
Greece conquered her savage victor. (Horace)*
Graviora manent - *Greater dangers await*
Gutta cavat lapidem, non vi sed saepe cadendo -
*The drop excavates the stone, not with force but by
falling often. (Ovid)*

H

Habeas corpus - *You must have the body, i.e. You must justify an imprisonment*

Habemus Papam - *We have a pope. (used at the announcement of a new pope)*

Habetis bona deum - *Have a nice day*

Hac lege - *With this law*

Haec olim meminisse ivvabit - *Time heals all things, i.e. Wounds, offenses*

Haec trutina errat - *There is something wrong with this scale*

Hannibal ante portas! - *Hannibal is at the doors! The enemy/danger is at the doors!*

Haud ignota loquor - *I say things that are known*

Helluo librorum - *A glutton for books. (bookworm)*

Heu! Tintinnuntius meus sonat! - *Darn! There goes my beeper!*

Heus, hic nos omnes in agmine sunt! - *Hey, we're all in line here!*

Hic et nunc - *Here and now*

Hic habitat felicitas - *Here dwells happiness*

Hic jacet (HJ) - *Here lies. (written on gravestones or tombs)*

Hic jacet sepultus (HJS) - *Here lies buried*

Hic puer est stultissimus omnium! - *This boy is the stupidest of all!*

Hinc illae lacrimae - *Hence these tears. (Terence)*

Historia est vitae magistra - *The history is the tutor of life*

Hoc erat in votis - *This was among my prayers*

Hoc est in votis - *This is in my prayers*

Hoc est verum et nihili nisi verum - *This is the truth and nothing but the truth*

Hoc est vivere bis vita posse priore frvi - *To live twice is to make useful profit from one's past. Experience is the best teacher, so learn from it*

Hoc natura est insitum, ut quem timueris, hunc semper oderis - *It's an innate thing to always hate the one we've learnt to fear*

Hoc tempore obsequium amicos, veritas odium parit - *In these days friends are won through flattery, the truth gives birth to hate. (Terence)*

Hocine bibo aut in eum digitos insero? - *Do I drink this or stick my fingers in it?*

Hodie mihi, cras tibi - *Today for me, tomorrow for you*

Homines libenter quod volunt credunt - *Men believe what they want to. (Terentius)*

Homines, dum docent, discunt - *Men learn while they teach. (Seneca)*

Homo doctvs is se semper divitias habet - *A learned man always has wealth within himself*

Homo homini lupus - *Man is a wolf to man*

Homo nudus cum nuda iacebat - *Naked they lay together, man and woman*

Homo praesumitur bonus donec probetur malus - *One is innocent until proven guilty*

Homo proponit, sed Deus disponit - *Man proposes, but God disposes*

Homo sum, humani nihil a me alienum puto - *I am human, therefore nothing human is strange to me*

Homo sum - *I am a man*

Homo vitae commodatus non donatus est - *Man has been lent to life, not given. (Pubilius Syrus)*

Honor virutis preamium - *Honour is the reward of*

virtue

Honores mutant mores - *The honours change the customs. (Power corrupts)*

Honoris causa (h.c.) - *As in doctorate, an honorary degree*

Horas non numero nisi serenas - *I count only the bright hours. (Inscription on ancient sundials)*

Horribile dictu - *Horrible to tell*

Horror vacui - *Fear of empty places*

Hostis hvmani generis - *Enemy of the human race*

Huc accedit zambonis! - *Here comes the Zamboni!*

Humum mandere - *To bite the dust*

Hunc tu caveto - *Beware of this man*

I

Ibidem (Ib.) - *In the same place. (in a book)*

Id certum est quod certum reddi potest - *That is certain that can be made certain*

Id est (i.e.) - *That is to say*

Id est mihi, id non est tibi! - *It is mine, not yours!*

Id imperfectum manet dum confectum erit - *It ain't over until it's over*

Id tibi praebet speciem lepidissimam! - *It looks great on you!*

Idem quod (i.q.) - *The same as*

Idem - *The same*

Iesus Nazarenus Rex Iudaeorum (INRI) - *Jesus of Nazareth, King of the Jews*

Ignis aurum probat, miseria fortes viros - *Life is not a bowl of cherries, or, literally, Fire tests gold; adversity tests strong men*

Ignis fatuus - *Foolish fire (will-o-the-wisp)*

Ignorantia juris neminem excusat - *Ignorance of*

the law excuses no one
Ignoratio elenchi - *An ignorance of proof*
Ignotus (ign.) - *Unknown*
Ille dolet vere, qui sine teste dolet - *He mourns honestly who mourns without witnesses. (Martialis)*
Ille mi par esse deo videtur - *He seems to me to be equal to a god. (Catullus)*
Illegitimis nil carborundum - *Don't let the bastards grind you down*
Illiud latine dici non potest - *You can't say that in Latin*
Illius me paenitet, dux - *Sorry about that, chief*
Imitatores, servum pecus! - *Imitators, you slavish crowd! (Horace)*
Imperator/Imperatrix (Imp.) - *Emperor/Empress*
Imperator - *Emperor*
Imperium et libertas - *Empire and liberty. (Cicero)*
Imperium in imperio - *An empire within an empire, i.e. A fifth column, a group of people within an nation's territory who owe allegiance to some other leader*
Imperium - *Absolute power*
Impossibilium nulla obligatio est - *Nobody has any obligation to the impossible. (Corpus Iuris Civilis)*
Imprimatur - *Let it be printed*
Imprimis - *In first place*
In absentia - *In one's absence*
In actu - *In practice*
In aere aedificare - *Build (castles) in the air. (St. Augustine)*
In aeternum - *For eternity*
In alio pediculum, in te ricinum non vides - *You*

see a louse on someone else, but not a tick on
yourself. (Petronius)
In articulo mortis - *At the moment of death*
In banco - *On the bench*
In camera - *In private chamber*
In capite - *In chief*
In cavda venenvm - *In the tail [is the] poison.*
Watch out for what you don't see
In curia - *In court*
In dentibus anticis frustrum magnum spiniciae
habes - *You have a big piece of spinach in your*
front teeth
In distans - *At a distance*
In dubiis non est agendum - *In dubious cases,*
you should not act
In dubio pro reo - *In doubt in favor of the accused.*
If there is a doubt about guiltiness, the judgement
has to be in favour of the accused
In dubio - *In doubt*
In esse - *In existence*
In excelsis - *In the highest*
In extenso - *At full length*
In extremis - *In extremity*
In fine - *At the end*
In flagrante delicto - *In the very act of committing*
an offence
In forma pauperis - *In the form of a poor person; in*
a humble or abject manner
In futuro - *In the future*
In gremio legis - *In the protection of the law*
In his ordo est ordinem non servare - *In this case*
the only rule is not obeying any rules
In hoc signo vinces - *In this sign, you will be*

victorious. (Eusebios)

In infinitum - *To infinity; without end*

In libris libertas - *In books (there is) freedom*

In limine - *On the threshold, at the very outset*

In loco parentis - *In the place of a parent*

In loco - *In the place of*

In magnis et voluisse sat est - *To once have wanted is enough in great deeds. (Propertius)*

In media res - *In or into the middle of a sequence of events. (Horace)*

In medias res - *Into the midst of things*

In medio stat virtus - *Virtue stands in the middle. Virtue is in the moderate, not the extreme position. (Horace)*

In medio tutissimus ibis - *In the middle of things you will go most safe. (Ovid)*

In memoriam - *To the memory of*

In necessariis unitas, in dubiis libertas, in omnibus caritas - *In necessary things unity, in doubtful things liberty, in all things charity*

In nomine Domini - *In the name of the Lord*

In nomine Patris et Filii et Spiritus Santi - *In the name of the Father and of the Son and of the Holy Spirit*

In nubibus - *In the clouds*

In nuce - *In a nutshell*

In omnia paratus - *Prepared for all things*

In ovo - *In the egg*

In pace, ut sapiens, aptarit idonea bello - *In peace, like a wise man, he appropriately prepares for war*

In pace - *In peace*

In pari materia - *Of like kind*

In partibus infidelium - *In parts inhabited by unbelievers*

In parvo - *In miniature*

In perpetuum - *For ever*

In personam - *Against the person*

In pleno - *In full*

In pontificalibus - *In the proper vestments of a pope or cardinal*

in posse - *In possibility*

In posterum - *Till the next day*

In praesenti - *At the present time*

In principio - *In the beginning*

In propria persona - *In person*

In puris naturalibus - *Completely naked*

In quaestione versare - *To be under investigation*

In re - *Refering to*

In rem - *Against the matter (property)*

In rerum natura - *In the nature of things*

In saecvla saecvlorvm - *For ages of ages forever*

In se - *In itself*

In silico - *By means of a computer simulation*

In silvam ne ligna feras - *Don't carry logs into the forest. (Horace)*

In situ - *In position*

In specie - *In kind; (a) in its own form and not in an equivalent (b) in coins and not in paper money*

In spiritu et veritate - *In spirit and truth. (Versio Vulgata)*

In statu quo - *In the same state*

In terrorem - *As a warning; in order to terrify others*

In totidem verbis - *In so many words*

In toto - *As a whole, absolutely, Completely*

In transitu - *In passing, on the way*

In usu - *In use*
In utero - *In the womb*
In vacuo - *In a vacuum or empty space*
In vinculis etiam audax - *In chains yet still bold (free)*
In vino veritas - *The truth is in wine. (A drunk person tells the truth)*
In virtute sunt multi ascensus - *There are many degrees in excellence. (Cicero)*
In vitro - *In a test tube (literally glass)*
In vivo - *In the living (thing)*
Incipit - *Begin here*
Incredibile dictu - *Incredible to say*
Index librorum prohibitorum - *Official list of forbidden books not to be read by Catholics*
Indulgentiam quaeso - *I ask your indulgence*
Infinitus est numerus stultorum - *Infinite is the number of fools*
Infra dignitatem (dig.) - *Undignified; beneath one's dignity*
Infra - *Below, underneath*
Inhumanitas omni aetate molesta est - *Inhumanity is harmful in every age. (Cicero)*
Iniqua nunquam regna perpetuo manent - *Stern masters do not reign long. (Seneca Philosophus)*
Iniuria non excusat iniuriam - *One wrong does not justify another*
Insanabile cacoethes scribendi - *An incurable passion to write. (Juvenal)*
Insculpsit - *He/she engraved it*
Instrumentum aeri temperando - *Airconditioner*
Insula gilliganis - *Gilligan's Island*
Integer vitae scelerisque purus - *Blameless of life*

and free from crime

Intellectum valde amat - *Love the intellect strongly. (St. Augustine)*

Intelligenti pauca - *Few words suffice for he who understands*

Intelligo me intelligere - *I understand that I understand. (St. Augustine)*

Inter alia - *Among other things*

Inter alios - *Amongst other people*

Inter arma silent leges - *In time of war, laws are silent*

Inter caecos regnat strabo - *Among blinds the squinting rules. (Erasmus)*

Inter caesa et porrecta - *There's many a slip twixt cup and lip*

Inter canum et lupum - *Between a dog and a wolf*

Inter nos - *Between ourselves*

Inter partes - *Made between two parties*

Inter se - *Between themselves*

Inter spem et metum - *Between hope and fear*

Inter vivos - *Between living (people)*

Interdum feror cupidine partium magnarum europe vincendarum - *Sometimes I get this urge to conquer large parts of Europe*

Interfice errorem, diligere errantem - *Kill the sin, love the sinner. (St. Augustine)*

Interregnvm - *Period between rules anarchy, lawlessnes*

Intra muros - *Within the walls*

Intra vires - *Within the power*

Inventas vitam iuvat excoluisse per artes - *Let us improve life through science and art. (Vergil)*

Ipsa qvidem pretivm virtvs sibi - *Virtue is its own*

reward

Ipsa scientia potestas est - *Knowledge itself is power. (Bacon)*

Ipsi dixit - *He himself said it. (Cicero)*

Ipsissima verba - *The exact words*

Ipso facto - *By that very fact*

Ipso iure - *By operation of the law*

Ira furor brevis est - *Anger is a brief insanity. (Horace)*

Ire fortiter quo nemo ante iit - *To boldly go where no man has gone before. (Star Trek)*

Isto pensitaris? - *You get paid for this crap?*

Ita erat quando hic adveni - *It was that way when I got here*

Ita est - *Yes./It is so*

Ite, misse est - *Go, the Mass is finished*

Iubilate Deo - *Rejoice in God*

Iunctis viribus - *By united efforts*

Iure divino - *By divine law*

Iure humano - *By human law*

Ius civile - *Civil law*

Ius gentium - *The law of nations*

Ius primae noctis - *The right of the first night*

Ivs est ars boni et aeqvi - *Law is the art of the good and the just*

Ivs gentivm - *Right of tribes law of nations*

J

Justitia omnibus - *Justice for all*

L

Labera lege - *Read my lips*

Labor omnia vincit - *Work conquers all things.*

(Virgil)
Labra lege - *Read my lips*
Lachryma Christi - *Christ's tears*
Lapsus alumni - *Error made*
Lapsus calami - *A slip of the pen*
Lapsus linguae - *A slip of the tongue*
Lapsus memoriae - *A slip of the memory*
Lapsus nivium! - *Avalanche!!*
Lares et penates - *Household gods*
Latet anguis in herba - *A snake lies in the grass.*
(Vergil)
Latine dictum - *Spoken in Latin*
Latine loqui coactus sum - *I have this compulsion to speak Latin*
Latro! fremo! - *Woof woof! Grrrr!*
Laudant illa, sed ista legunt - *Some (writing) is praised, but other is read. (Martialis)*
Laudatores temporis acti - *Praisers of time past*
Laus Deo - *Praise be to God*
Lavdem virtvtis necessitati damvs - *We give to necessity the praise of virtue finding the benefit in what's needful*
Lectori Salutem (L.S.) - *Greetings to the reader*
Lectio brevior lectio potior - *The shortest reading is the more probable reading*
Lector benevole - *Kind reader*
Legatus a latere - *Advisor from the side*
Lege atque lacrima - *Read 'em and weep*
Lege et lacrima - *Read it and weep*
Legum servi sumus ut liberi esse possimus - *We are slaves of the law so that we may be able to be free. (Cicero)*
Leve fit, quod bene fertur, onus - *The burden is*

46

made light which is borne well. (Ovid)
Lex clavatoris designati rescindenda est - *The designated hitter rule has got to go*
Lex domicilii - *The law of a person's home country*
Lex fori - *The law of the forum (country)*
Lex loci - *The law of the place*
Lex malla, lex nulla - *A bad law is no law. (St. Thomas Aquinas)*
Lex non scripta - *The unwritten (common) law*
Lex scripta - *The written law*
Lex talionis - *The law of revenge*
Libenter homines id quod volunt credunt - *Men gladly believe that which they wish for. (Caesar)*
Liberae sunt nostrae cogitationes - *Our thoughts are free. (Cicero)*
Liberate te ex inferis - *Save yourself from hell*
Libertas inaestimabilis res est - *Liberty is a thing beyond all price. (Corpus Iuris Civilis)*
Liberum arbitrium - *Free will*
Libra solidus denarius (L.S.D.) - *Pounds, shillings, pence*
Licentia liquendi - *Liberty of speaking*
Licentia poetica - *Poetic licence. (Seneca)*
Licet - *It is allowed*
Lingua franca - *French tongue - the common or universal language*
Literati - *Men of letters*
Litoralis - *Beach bum*
Litterae humaniores - *The humanities*
Loco citato (lc) - *In the passage just quoted*
Locum tenens - *One occupying the place (used as an English noun meaning 'deputy')*
Locus classicus - *The most authoritative source,*

Classical passage
Locus delicti - *The scene of the crime*
Locus desperatus - *A hopeless passage*
Locus enim est principum generationis rerum - *For place is the origin of things. (Roger Bacon)*
Locus in quo - *The place in which something happens*
Locus poenitentiae - *A place for repentance*
Locus sigilli (l.s.) - *The place of the seal*
Locus standi - *Place of standing*
Longo intervallo - *After a long gap*
Loquitur (loq.) - *He/she speaks*
Luctor et emergo - *I struggle but I'll survive*
Luke sum ipse patrem te - *Luke, I am your father. (Star Wars)*
Lumen naturale - *Natural light*
Lupus est homo homini - *Man is wolf to man*
Lupus in fabula - *The wolf in the tale (i.e. Speak of the wolf, and he will come) (Terence)*
Lusus naturae - *A freak of nature*
Lux et veritas - *Light and Truth*
Lux mundi - *The light of the world*

M

Machina improba! Vel mihi ede potum vel mihi redde nummos meos! - *You infernal machine! Give me a beverage or give me my money back!*
Maecenas atavis edite regibus - *Maecenas, born of monarch ancestors. (Horace)*
Magister artis ingeniique largitor venter - *Necessity is the mother of all invention*
Magister Artium (MA) - *Master of arts*
Magister mundi sum! - *I am the master of the universe!*

Magna charta - *Great paper*

Magna cum laude - *With great honour or academic distinction*

Magna res est vocis et silentii temperamentum - *The great thing is to know when to speak and when to keep quiet*

Magnas inter oper inops - *A pauper in the midst of wealth. (Horace)*

Magnificat - *It magnifies*

Magnum bonum - *A great good*

Magnum opus - *Great work, the major work of one's life*

Magnus frater spectat te - *Big Brother is watching you*

Maior risus, acrior ensis: quadragesima octava regula quaesitus - *The bigger the smile, the sharper the knife: the 48th rule of acquisition*

Mala fide - *In bad faith (something which is done fraudulently)*

Male parta male dilabuntur - *What has been wrongly gained is wrongly lost. (Ill-gotten gains seldom prosper.) (Cicero)*

Malum consilium quod mutari non potest - *It's a bad plan that can't be changed. (Publilius Syrus)*

Malum prohibitum - *A prohibited wrong. A crime that society decides is wrong for some reason, not inherently evil*

Malum quidem nullum esse sine aliquo bono - *There is, to be sure, no evil without something good. (Pliny the Elder)*

Manus in mano - *Hand in hand*

Manus manum lavat - *One hand washes the other. The favor for the favor. (Petronius)*

Mare clausum - *A closed sea*

Mare liberum - *An open sea*

Mare nostrum - *Our sea. (Mediterranean)*

Margaritas ante porcos - *Pearls before swine. To give something valuable to someone not respecting it*

Mater artium necessitas - *Necessity is the mother of invention*

Mater dolorosa - *Sorrowful mother. (Virgin Mary)*

Mater memento mori - *Remember your mortality*

Mater tua criceta fuit, et pater tuo redoluit bacarum sambucus - *Your mother was a hamster and your father smelt of elderberries*

Mater - *Mother*

Materfamilias - *Mother of family*

Materia medica - *Medical matter*

Materiam superabat opus - *The workmanship was better than the subject matter. (Ovid)*

Maxima debetur puero reverentia - *We owe the greatest respect to a child*

Maximus in minimis - *Great in little things*

Me fallit - *I do not know*

Me iudice - *I being judge; in my judgement*

Me oportet propter praeceptum te nocere - *I'm going to have to hurt you on principle*

Me transmitte sursum, caledoni! - *Beam me up, Scotty!*

Mea culpa - *Through my fault*

Mea maxima culpa - *Through my very great fault*

Mea mihi conscientia pluris est quam omnium sermo - *My conscience means more to me than all speech. (Cicero)*

Medice, cura te ipsum! - *Physician, heal thyself!*

(Versio Vulgata)

Medici graviores morbos asperis remediis curant - *Doctors cure the more serious diseases with harsh remedies. (Curtius Rufus)*

Medicus curat, natura sanat - *The physician treats, nature cures*

Medio tutissimus ibis - *You will go safest in the middle. (Moderation in all things) (Ovid)*

Mei capilli sunt flagrantes - *My hair is on fire*

Meliora cogito - *I strive for the best*

Melitae amor - *Love of Malta*

Melius est praevenire quam praeveniri - *Better to forestall than to be forestalled*

Melius frangi quam flecti - *It is better to break than to bend*

Melius tarde, quam nunquam - *Better late than never*

Mellita, domi adsum - *Honey, I'm home*

Memento mori - *Remember that you must die*

Memento vivere - *A reminder of life (literally remember that you have to live)*

Memorabilia - *Memorable things*

Memorandum - *A note of; a thing to be remembered*

Memoria in aeterna - *In everlasting remembrance*

Memoriter - *From memory*

Mendacem memorem esse oportet - *A liar needs a good memory. (Quintilianus)*

Mens agitat molem - *The mind moves the matter. (Vergil)*

Mens rea - *Guilty mind*

Mens regnum bona possidet - *An honest heart is a kingdom in itself. (Seneca)*

Mens sana in corpore sano - *A sound mind in a sound body. (Juvenalis)*
Mens sibi conscia recti - *A mind conscious of its rectitude*
Meum cerebrum nocet - *My brain hurts*
Meum pactum dictum - *My word is my bond*
Mihi cura futuri - *My concern is the future*
Mihi ignosce. Cum homine de cane debeo congredi - *Excuse me. I've got to see a man about a dog*
Millennium (millennia) - *A thousand year period*
Minime senuisti! - *You haven't aged a bit!*
Minus habens - *Absentminded*
Mirabile dictu - *Wonderful to say/relate. (Vergil)*
Mirabile visu - *Wonderful to behold*
Miserere - *Have mercy*
Missa solemnis - *Solemn Mass. (high Mass)*
Mittimus - *We send (to prison)*
Modus agendi - *Manner of operation*
Modus operandi (m.o.) - *Way of operating*
Modus vivendi - *Way of living*
Monstra mihi pecuniam! - *Show me the money!*
Moratorium - *A delay*
Morituri te salutant - *Those who are about to die salute you*
Mors ultima linea rerum est - *Death is everything's final limit. (Horace)*
Mors ultima ratio - *Death is the final accounting*
Mortvi non mordant - *Dead me don't bite; Dead men tell no tale*
Motu proprio - *Of one's own initiative*
Mulier taceat in ecclesia - *Let the woman be silent in church. (Paul)*

Multi famam, conscientiam pauci verentur - *Many fear their reputation, few their conscience. (Pliny)*
Multis post annis - *Many years later*
Multum in parvo - *Much in little. (small but significant)*
Multun, non multa - *Much, not many (quality not quantity)*
Mundus vult decipi, ergo decipiatur - *The world wants to be deceived, so let it be deceived!*
Mundus vult decipi - *The world wants to be deceived*
Munit haec et altera vincit - *One defends and the other conquers*
Mus uni non fidit antro - *A mouse does not rely on just one hole. (Plautus)*
Musica delenit bestiam feram - *Music soothes the savage beast*
Mutatis mutandis - *The necessary changes having been made*
Mutato nomine - *The name being changed*
Mvlti svnt vocati, pavci vero electi - *Many are called [but] few are chosen*
Mvndvs vvlt decipi - *The world wishes to be deceived there's a sucker born every minute*
Mvtatis mvtandis - *The things that ought to have changed having been changed with the necessary substitutions having been made*

N

Nam et ipsa scientia potestas es - *Knowledge is power. (Sir Francis Bacon)*
Nascentes morimur - *From the moment we are born, we begin to die*

Natale solum - *Native soil*

Natura abhorret a vacua - *Nature abhors a vacuum*

Natura in minima maxima - *Nature is the greatest in the smallest things*

Natura nihil fit in frustra - *Nature does nothing in vain*

Natura, artis magistra - *Nature, the mistress of art*

Naturam expellas furca, tamen usque recurret - *You can drive nature out with a pitchfork but she always comes back*

Navigare necesse est - *To sail is necessary*

Ne auderis delere orbem rigidum meum! - *Don't you dare erase my hard disk!*

Ne cede malis - *Yield not to evils*

Ne feceris ut rideam - *Don't make me laugh*

Ne humanus crede - *Trust no human*

Ne nimium - *Not too much*

Ne plus ultra - *No further. Impassable obstacle*

Ne quid nimis - *Nothing in excess. (Terence)*

Nec laudas nisi mortuos poetas: tanti non est, ut placeam, perire - *If only dead poets are praised, I'd rather go unsung*

Nec mortem effugere quisquam nec amorem potest - *No one is able to flee from death or love*

Nec possum tecum vivere, nec sine te - *I am able to live / I can live neither with you, nor without you. (Martial)*

Nec verbum verbo curabis reddere fidus interpres - *As a true translator you will take care not to translate word for word. (Horace)*

Necesse est multos timeat quem multi timent - *He must fear many, whom many fear. (Laberius)*

Necessitas non habet legem - *Necessity knows no law*

Negotium populo romano melius quam otium committi - *The Roman people understand work better than leisure*

Nemine contradicente (nem. con.) - *With no one speaking in opposition. Unanimously*

Nemine dissentiente (nem. diss.) - *With no one disagreeing*

Nemo ante mortem beatus - *Nobody is blessed before his death. We never know what is future preparing for us!*

Nemo autem regere potest nisi qui et regi - *Moreover, there is no one who can rule unless he can be ruled. (Seneca)*

Nemo dat quod non habet - *No one gives what he does not have*

Nemo gratis mendax - *No man lies freely. A person with no reason to lie is telling the truth*

Nemo hic adest illius nominis - *There is no one here by that name*

Nemo liber est qui corpori servit - *No one is free who is a slave to his body*

Nemo malus felix - *No bad man is lucky. (Juvenal)*

Nemo me impune lacessit - *No one provokes me with impunity. (motto of the Kings of Scotland)*

Nemo nisi mors - *Nobody except death (will part us). (Inscription in the wedding ring of the Swedish Queen Katarina Jagellonica)*

Nemo propheta in patria sua - *No one is considered a prophet in his hometown/homeland*

Nemo repente fuit turpissimus - *No one ever became thoroughly bad in one step. (Juvenal)*

Nemo risum praebuit, qui ex se coepit - *Nobody is laughed at, who laughs at himself. (Seneca)*

Nemo saltat sobrius nisi forte insanit - *Nobody dances sober unless he's insane*

Nemo saltat sobrius - *No man dances sober*

Nemo sine vitio est - *No one is without fault. (Seneca the Elder)*

Nemo surdior est quam is qui non audiet - *No man is more deaf than he who will not hear*

Nemo timendo ad summum pervenit locum - *No man by fearing reaches the top. (Syrus)*

Nervos belli, pecuniam. (Nervus rerum.) - *The nerve of war, money. (The nerve of things.) (Cicero)*

Nescio quid dicas - *I don't know what you're talking about*

Neutiquam erro - *I am not lost*

Nihil ad rem - *Nothing to do with the point*

Nihil agere delectat - *It is pleasant to do nothing. (Cicero)*

Nihil aliud scit necessitas quam vincere - *Necesssity knows nothing else but victory. (Syrus)*

Nihil curo de ista tua stulta superstitione - *I'm not interested in your dopey religious cult*

Nihil declaro - *I have nothing to declare*

Nihil est ab omni parte beatum - *Nothing is good in every part. (Horace)*

Nihil est incertius volgo - *Nothing is more uncertain than the (favour of the) crowd. (Cicero)*

Nihil est miserum nisi cum putes - *Nothing is unfortunate if you don't consider it unfortunate. (Boethius)*

Nihil est--In vita priore ego imperator romanus fui - *That's nothing--in a previous life I was a Roman*

Emperor

Nihil obstat - *Nothing stands in the way*

Nihil sub sole novum - *Nothing new under the sun*

Nihil tam munitum quod non expugnari pecunia possit - *No fort is so strong that it cannot be taken with money. (Cicero)*

Nihil - *Nothing*

Nil actum credens dum quid superesset agendum - *Thinking nothing done, while anything was yet to do*

Nil actum reputa si quid superest agendum - *Don't consider that anything has been done if anything is left to be done. (Lucan)*

Nil admirari - *To admire nothing. (Horace)*

Nil agit exemplum, litem quod lite resolvit - *Not much worth is an example that solves one quarrel with another. (Horace)*

Nil desperandum! - *Never despair! (Horace)*

Nil homini certum est - *Nothing is certain for man. (Ovid)*

Nil sine numine - *Nothing without the Divine Will*

Nill illigitimi carborundum - *Do not let the bastards get you down*

Nisi credideritis, non intelligetis - *Unless you will have believed, you will not understand. (St. Augustine)*

Nisi prius - *Unles previously*

Nisi - *Unless*

Nolens volens - *Whether one likes it or not; willing or unwilling*

Noli equi dentes inspicere donati - *Do not look a gift horse in the mouth. (St. Jerome)*

Noli me tangere! - *Don't touch me! (Versio Vulgata)*

Noli me voca, ego te vocabo - *Don't call me. I'll call you*

Noli nothis permittere te terere - *Dont let the bastards get you down*

Noli simul flare sobereque - *Don't whistle and drink at the same time*

Noli turbare circulos meos! - *Don't upset my calculations! (Archimedes)*

Nolite id cogere, cape malleum majorem - *Don't force it, get a bigger hammer*

Nolle prosequi - *Do not pursue*

Nolo contendere - *I do not wish to contend*

Nomen est omen - *The name is the sign*

Nomina stultorum parietibus haerent - *The names of foolish persons adhere to walls (Fools names and fools faces are often seen in public places.)*

Nominatim - *By name*

Non bis in idem - *Not twice for the same thing*

Non calor sed umor est qui nobis incommodat - *It's not the heat, it's the humidity*

Non compos mentis - *Not in possession of one's senses*

Non curo. Si metrum non habet, non est poema - *I don't care. If it doesn't rhyme, it isn't a poem*

Non erravi perniciose! - *I did not commit a fatal error!*

Non est ad astra mollis e terris via - *There is no easy way from the earth to the stars. (Seneca)*

Non est ei similis - *There is no one like him*

Non est mea culpa - *It's not my fault*

Non est vivere sed valere vita est - *Life is not being alive but being well (life is more than just* *being alive)*

Non Gradus Anus Rodentum! - *Not Worth A Rats Ass!*

Non ignara mals, miseris svccvrrere disco - *No stranger to misfortune [myself] I learn to relieve the sufferings [of others*

Non illigitamus carborundum - *Don't let the bastards grind you down*

Non licet - *It is not allowed*

Non liquet - *It is not clear*

Non mihi, non tibi, sed nobis - *Not for you, not for me, but for us - the foundation of a good relationship*

Non mortem timemus, sed cogitationem mortis - *We do not fear death, but the thought of death. (Seneca)*

Non multa, sed multum - *Not many, but much. (Meaning, not quantity but quality) (Plinius)*

Non nobis, Domine - *Not unto us, O Lord*

Non omne quod licet honestum est - *Not everything that is permitted is honest. (Corpus Iuris Civilis)*

Non omne quod nitet aurum est - *Not all that glitters is gold*

Non omnes qui habemt citharam sunt citharoedi - *Not all those who own a musical instrument are musicians. (Bacon)*

Non omnia moriar - *Not all of me will die. (Horace)*

Non omnia possumus omnes - *Not all of us are able to do all things (We can't all do everything.) (Virgil)*

Non omnis moriar - *Not all of me will die. (his works would live forever) (Horace)*

Non placet - *It does not please*

Non plaudite. Modo pecuniam jacite - *Don't applaud. Just throw money*

Non plus ultra! (Nec plus ultra!) - *Nothing above that!*

Non prosequitur - *He does not proceed*

Non quis, sed quid - *Not who, but what*

Non rape me si placet - *Please don't rob me*

Non scholae sed vitae discimus - *We do not learn for school, but for life. (Seneca)*

Non semper erit aestas - *It will not always be summer (be prepared for hard times)*

Non sequitur - *It does not follow*

Non serviam - *I will not serve*

Non sibi sed suis - *Not for one's self but for one's people*

Non sibi, sed patriae - *Not for you, but for the fatherland*

Non sum pisces - *I am not a fish*

Non sum qualis eram - *I am not what / of what sort I was (I'm not what I used to be.)*

Non teneas aurum totum quod splendet ut aurum - *Do not take as gold everything that shines like gold*

Non timetis messor - *Don't Fear the Reaper*

Non uno die roma aedificata est - *Rome was not built in one day (either)*

Non ut edam vivo, sed vivam edo - *I do not live to eat, but eat to live. (Quintilianus)*

Non vereor ne illam me amare hic potuerit resciscere; quippe haud etiam quicquam inepte feci - *I don't think anyone knows I love the girl; I haven't done anything really silly yet*

Non, mihi ignosce, credo me insequentem esse -

No, excuse me, I believe I'm next

Nonne amicus certus in re incerta cernitur? - *A friend in need is a friend in deed. (our equivalent)*

Nonne de novo eboraco venis? - *You're from New York, aren't you?*

Nonne macescis? - *Have you lost weight?*

Nosce te ipsum - *Know thyself. (Inscription at the temple of Apollo in Delphi.)*

Nota bene (nb.) - *Note well. Observe carefully*

Novus homo - *A new Man; a man who was the first in his family to be elected to an office*

Novus ordo saeculorum - *A new order of ages*

Novus ordo seclorum - *A new order for the ages. (appears on the U.S. one-dollar bill)*

Nulla avarita sine poena est - *There is no avarice without penalty. (Seneca)*

Nulla dies sine linea - *Not a day without a line. Do something every day! (Apeles, Greek painter)*

Nulla regula sine exceptione - *There is no rule/law without exception*

Nulla res carius constat quam quae precibus empta est - *Nothing is so expensive as that which you have bought with pleas. (Seneca)*

Nulla vit melior quam bona - *There's no life better than a good life*

Nulli expugnabilis hosti - *Conquered By No Enemy. (motto of Gibraltar)*

Nulli secundus - *Second to none*

Nullius in verba - *(Rely) on the words on no one. (Horace)*

Nullo metro compositum est - *It doesn't rhyme*

Nullum crimen sine lege, nulla poena sine lege - *No crime and no punishment without a (pre-existing)* *law*

Nullum est iam dictum quod non dictum sit prius - *Nothing is said that hasn't been said before. (Terence)*

Nullum gratuitum prandium - *There is no free lunch!*

Nullum magnum ingenium sine mixtura dementiae - *There is no one great ability without a mixture of madness*

Nullum saeculum magnis ingeniis clausum est - *No generation is closed to great talents. (Seneca)*

Nullus est instar domus - *There is no place like home*

Nullus est liber tam malus ut non aliqua parte prosit - *There is no book so bad that it is not profitable on some part. (Pliny the Younger)*

Numen - *Divine power*

Numero pondere et mensura Deus omnia condidit - *God created everything by number, weight and measure. (Isaac Newton)*

Numerus clausus - *A restricted number*

Nummus americanus - *Greenback. ($US)*

Numquam aliud natura, aliud sapientia dicit - *Never does nature say one thing and wisdom say another*

Numquam non paratus - *Never unprepared*

Numquam se minus solum quam cum solus esset - *You are never so little alone as when you are alone. (Cicero)*

Nunc dimittis - *Now let depart*

Nunc est bibendum - *Now we must drink. (Horace)*

Nvdvm pactvm - *A nude pact an invalid agreement a contract with illusory benefits or without*

consideration hence unenforceable
Nvllvm qvod tetiget non ornavit - *He touched none he did not adorn - not simply 'the Midas touch', or 'he left things better than he found them', but a tribute to a Renaissance man*
Nvnc avt nvnqvam - *Now or never*
Nvnc dimittis - *Now let [thy servant] depart - generally any permission to go, specifically to express one's readiness to depart or die*
Nvnc pro tvnc - *Now for then retroactive*

O

O curas hominum! O quantum est in rebus inane! - *Ah, human cares! Ah, how much futility in the world! (Lucilius)*
O di immortales! - *Good heavens! (uttered by Cicero on the Senate floor)*
O diem praeclarum! - *Oh, what a beautiful day!*
O praeclarum custodem ovium lupum! - *An excellent protector of sheep, the wolf! (Cicero)*
O quam cito transit gloria mundi! - *O how quickly passes the glory of the world!*
O sancta simplicitas! - *Oh, holy simplicity! (Jan Hus)*
O tempora, O mores! - *Oh, the times! Oh, the morals! (Cicero)*
O! Plus! Perge! Aio! Hui! Hem! - *Oh! More! Go on! Yes! Ooh! Ummm!*
Obesa cantavit - *The fat lady has sung*
Obiit (ob.) - *He/she died*
Obiter (ob.) - *In passing*
Obiter dictum - *Something said in passing - parenthetical remark*
Oblitus sum perpolire clepsydras! - *I forgot to*

polish the clocks!

Obscurum per obscurius - *The obscure by means of the more obscure*

Obsta principiis - *Resist the beginnings - Nip it in the bud*

Occasio aegre offertur, facile amittitur - *Opportunity is offered with difficulty, lost with ease. (Publius Syrus)*

Occasio facit furem - *Opportunity makes a thief*

Oderint dum metuant - *Let them hate provided that they fear. (Seneca)*

Odi et amo - *I hate (her), and I love (her) (Catullus)*

Odium theologicum - *Theological hatred. (a special name for the hatred generated in theological disputes)*

Olevm addere camino - *To pour fuel on the stove adding gasoline to a fire*

Olevm perdisti - *You have lost oil you've wasted your time on this criticism for a misallocation of resources*

Olim habeas eorum pecuniam, numquam eam reddis: prima regula quaesitus - *Once you have their money, you never give it back: the 1st rule of acquisiton*

Olim - *Formerly*

Omne ignotum pro magnifico est - *We have great notions of everything unknown. (Tacitus)*

Omne initium est difficile - *Every beginning is difficult*

Omne trium perfectum - *Everything that comes in threes is perfect*

Omne tvlit pvnctvm qvi miscvit vtile dvlci - *[he] has gained every point who has combined [the]* *useful [with the] agreeable*

Omnes aequo animo parent ubi digni imperant - *All men cheerfully obey where worthy men rule. (Syrus)*

Omnes deteriores svmvs licentia - *Too much freedom debases us*

Omnes lagani pistrinae gelate male sapiunt - *All frozen pizzas taste lousy*

Omnes una manet nox - *The same night awaits us all. (Horace)*

Omnes vulnerant, ultima necat - *All (hours) wound, the last kills. (inscription on solar clocks)*

Omnia iam fient quae posse negabam - *Everything which I used to say could not happen will happen now. (Ovid)*

Omnia mea mecum porto - *All that is mine, I carry with me. (My wisdom is my greatest wealth) (Cicero)*

Omnia mihi lingua graeca sunt - *It's all Greek to me*

Omnia mors aequat - *Death equals all things*

Omnia munda mundis - *Everything is pure to pure ones*

Omnia mutantur nos et mutamur in illis - *All things change, and we change with them*

Omnia mutantur, nihil interit - *Everything changes, nothing perishes. (Ovid)*

Omnia mutantur, nos et mutamur in illis - *All things are changing, and we are changing with them*

Omnia vincit amor - *Love conquers all*

Omnia vincit amor; et nos cedamus amori - *Love conquers all things; let us too surrender to love. (Vergil)*

Omnium gatherum - *Assortment*

Omnium rerum principia parva sunt - *Everything has a small beginning. (Cicero)*
Onus probandi - *The burden of proof*
Opere citato (op. cit.) - *In the work just quoted*
Optimis parentibus - *To my excellent parents. A common dedication in a book*
Optimus magister, bonus liber - *The best teacher is a good book*
Opus Dei - *The work of God*
Ora et labora - *Pray and work. (St. Benedict)*
Ora pro nobis - *Pray for us*
Oratvr fit, poeta nascitvr - *An orator is made [but] a poet is born*
Orbes volantes exstare - *Flying saucers are real*
Orbiter dictum/dicta - *Said by the way (miscellaneous remarks)*
Orcae ita - *Pretty straightforward*
Ore rotundo - *With full voice*
Osculare pultem meam! - *Kiss my grits!*

P
Pace tua - *With your consent*
Pace - *By leave of*
Pacta sunt servanda - *Agreements are to be kept. (Cicero)*
Pactum serva - *Keep the faith*
Pallida mors - *Pale Death. (Horace)*
Palmam qui meruit ferat - *Let him who has earned it bear the reward*
Panem et circenses - *Bread and circuses. Food and games to keep people happy. (Juvenalis)*
Par pare refero - *I return like for like tit for tat retaliation*
Parens patriae - *Parent of the country*

Pares cvm paribvs - *Like persons with like persons. Birds of a feather flock together*

Pari passu - *With equal pace - moving together*

Pars maior lacrimas ridet et intus habet - *You smile at your tears but have them in your heart. (Martialis)*

Particeps criminis - *Partner in crime*

Parturient montes, nascetur ridiculus mus - *Mountains will be in labour, and an absurd mouse will be born. (all that work and nothing to show for it)*

Parva leves capiunt animas - *Small things occupy light minds (small things amuse small minds)*

Parva scintilla saepe magnam flamam excitat - *The small sparkle often initiates a large flame*

Passim - *All through*

Pater familias - *Father of the family*

Pater historiae - *The father of history*

Pater Noster - *Our Father (The first words of the Lord's Prayer in Latin)*

Pater patriae - *Father of the country*

Patria est communis omnium parens - *Our native land is the common parent of us all. (Cicero)*

Patris est filius - *He is his father's son*

Paucis verbis, quid est deconstructionismus? - *What, in a nutshell, is deconstructionism?*

Paucis verbis - *In a few words*

Pavesco, pavesco - *I'm shaking, I'm shaking*

Pavpertas omnivm artivm repertrix - *Poverty [is the] inventor of all the arts necessity is the mother of invention*

Pax et bonum! - *Peace and salvation!*

Pax tecum - *May peace be with you (Singular)*

Pax vobiscum - *May peace be with you (Plural)*

Pax - *Peace*

Peccatum tacituritatis - *Sin of silence*

Peccavi - *I have sinned*

Peculium - *Property*

Pecunia in arbotis non crescit - *Money does not grow on trees*

Pecunia non olet - *Money has no smell. Money doesn't stink. (don't look a gift horse in the mouth) (Vespasianus)*

Pecvniate obedivnt omnia - *All things obey money. Money makes the world go round*

Pede poena claudo - *Punishment comes limping. Retribution comes slowly, but surely. (Horace)*

Pendente lite - *While a suit is pending*

Penetalia mentis - *The innermost recesses of the mind. Heart of hearts*

Per accidens - *By Accident*

Per angusta in augusta - *Through difficulties to great things*

Per annum (p.a.) - *Yearly*

Per ardua ad astra - *Through difficulties to the stars*

Per aspera ad astra - *Through the thorns to the stars*

Per capita - *Per head*

Per cent (per centum) - *Per hundred*

Per contra - *On the contrary*

Per diem - *Per day; daily allowance*

Per fas et nefas - *Through right or wrong*

Per impossibile - *As is impossible a way to qualify a proposition that cannot ever be true*

Per mensem - *Monthly*

Per procurationem (per pro) - *By delegation to*

Per se - *By or in itself*

Per varios usus artem experientia fecit - *Through different exercises practice has brought skill. (Manilius)*

Perfer et obdura; dolor hic tibi proderit olim - *Be patient and tough; some day this pain will be useful to you. (Ovid)*

Periculum in mora - *There is danger in delay. (Livy)*

Perpetuo vincit qui utitur clementia - *He is forever victor who employs clemency. (Syrus)*

Perpetuum mobile - *Perpetual motion*

Perscriptio in manibus tabellariorum est - *The check is in the mail*

Persona (non) grata - *(un)welcome person*

Pessimum genus inimicorum laudantes - *Flatterers are the worst type of enemies*

Pessimus inimicorum genus, laudantes - *The worst kind of enemies, those who can praise. (Tacitus)*

Petitio principii - *An assumption at the start*

Philosophum non facit barba! - *The beard does not define a philosopher. (Plutarch)*

Pictor ignotus - *Painter unknown*

Pinxit - *He/she painted it*

Pistrix! Pistrix! - *Shark! Shark!*

Placebo - *I will please. Medical expression for remedies with no medical effect, which improve one's medical condition only because one believes they do*

Placet - *It pleases*

Pleno iure - *With full authority*

Pluralitas non est ponenda sine neccesitate -

Entities should not be multiplied unnecessarily

Plusque minusque - *More or less*

Plvres crapvla qvam gladivs - *Drunkeness [kills] more than the sword. As true today on the road as it ever was*

Poeta nascitur, non fit - *The poet is born, not made*

Poli, poli, di umbuendo - *Slowly, Slowly we will get there*

Pone ubi sol non lucet! - *Put it where the sun don't shine!*

Posse (posse comitatus) - *The power of the country*

Possunt quia posse videntur - *They can because they think they can*

Post bellum - *After the war*

Post coitem - *After sexual intercourse*

Post factum - *After the fact*

Post hoc ergo propter hoc - *After this, therefore because of this*

Post hoc - *After this*

Post meridiem (p.m.) - *After midday*

Post mortem - *After death. (nowadays, the autopsy performed by a coroner)*

Post obitum - *After death*

Post partum - *After childbirth*

Post proelia praemia - *After the battles come the rewards*

Post scriptum (ps) - *After what has been written*

Post tenebras lux - *After the darkness, light*

Postatem obscuri lateris nescitis - *You do not know the power of the dark side*

Potes currere sed te occulere non potes - *You*

can run, but you can't hide
Potest ex casa magnus vir exire - *A great man can come from a hut. (Seneca)*
Potestatem obscuri lateris nescis - *You don't know the power of the dark side. (Star Wars)*
Potius mori quam foedari - *Rather to die than to be dishonoured (death before dishonour)*
Potius sero quam numquam - *It's better late than never. (Livy)*
Praemonitus, pramunitus - *Forewarned, forearmed*
Praetio prudentia praestat - *Prudence supplies a reward*
Prehende uxorem meam, sis! - *Take my wife, please!*
Prescriptio in manibus tabellariorium est - *The check is in the mail*
Pretium iustum est - *The Price is Right*
Prima facie - *At first sight; on the face of it. (in law, an obvious case that requires no further proof)*
Primum mobile - *Prime mover*
Primum non nocere - *The first thing is to do no harm. (Hippocratic oath)*
Primum viveri deinde philosophari - *Live before you philosophize, or Leap before you look*
Primus inter pares - *First among equals*
Principiis obsta - *Resist the beginnings*
Pro bono (pro bono publico) - *For the good of the public*
Pro di immortales! - *Good Heavens!*
Pro et contra - *For and against*
Pro forma - *As a matter of formality*
Pro hac vice - *For this occaision*

Pro memoria - *For a memorial*

Pro nunc - *For now*

Pro opportunitate - *As circumstances allow*

Pro patria - *For one's country*

Pro rata - *In proportion to the value. (per hour for example)*

Pro re nata (prn) - *For an occasion as it arises*

Pro se - *On one's own behalf*

Pro tanto - *So far*

Pro tempore (pro tem.) - *For the time being*

Probae esti in segetem sunt deteriorem datae fruges, tamen ipsae suaptae enitent - *A good seed, planted even in poor soil, will bear rich fruit by its own nature. (Accius)*

Probatum est - *It has been proved*

Probitas laudatur et alget - *Honesty is praised and left in the cold. (Juvenal)*

Promotor fidei - *Promoter of the faith*

Promoveatur ut amoveatur - *Let him be promoted to get him out of the way*

Propino fibi salutem! - *Cheers!*

Proprium humani ingenii est odisse quem laeseris - *It is human nature to hate a person whom you have injured*

Proxime accessit - *He/she came close*

Proximo (prox.) - *Of the next month*

Proximus sum egomet mihi - *I am closest to myself. (Charity begins at home.) (Terence)*

Pueri pueri, pueri puerilia tractant - *Children are children, (therefore) children do childish things*

Pulvis et umbra sumus - *We are dust and shadow. (Horace)*

Purgamentum init, exit purgamentum - *Garbage*

in, garbage out

Puris omnia pura - *To the pure all things are pure*

Puri sermonis amator - *A lover of pure speech. (Terence)*

Q

Qua - *In so far as*

Quad nesciunt eos non interficiet - *What they don't know won't kill them*

Quandoquidem inter nos sanctissima divitiarum maiestas, esti funesta pecunia templo nondum habitas - *Among us, the god most revered is Wealth, but so far it has no temple of its own*

Quae nocent, saepe docent - *What hurts, often instructs. One learns by bitter/adverse experience*

Quae vide (qqv) - *See these things*

Quaere verum - *Seek the truth*

Quaere - *(You might) ask. Used to introduce questions, usually rhetorical or tangential questions*

Qualem blennum! - *What a doofus!*

Qualem muleirculam! - *What a bimbo!*

Qualis pater talis filius - *As is the father, so is the son; like father, like son*

Quam bene vivas refert, non quam diu - *The important thing isn't how long you live, but how well you live. (Seneca)*

Quam se ipse amans-sine rivali! - *Himself loving himself so much-without a rival! (Cicero)*

Quam terribilis est haec hora - *How fearful is this hour*

Quandam - *Formally*

Quando omni flunkus moritatus - *When all else fails play dead*

Quantum materiae materietur marmota monax si

marmota monax materiam possit materiari? - *How much wood would a woodchuck chuck if a woodchuck could chuck wood?*

Quantum meruit - *As much as he/she deserved*

Quantum sufficit (qs) - *As much as suffices*

Quaque mane (qm) - *Every morning*

Quaque nocte (qn) - *Every night*

Quasi - *As if*

Quater in die (Q.I.D) - *Take four times a day*

Quem di diligunt, adolescens moritur - *Whom the gods love die young. (only the good die young)*

Quemadmodum possums scire utrum vere simus an solum sentiamus nos esse? - *How are we to know whether we actually exist or only think we exist?*

Quemadmoeum gladis nemeinum occidit, occidentis telum est - *A sword is never a killer, it's a tool in the killer's hands. (Seneca)*

Qui bene cantat, bis orat - *He who sings well, prays twice*

Qui bono? - *Who benfits?*

Qui dedit benificium taceat; narret qui accepit - *Let him who has done a good deed be silent; let him who has received it tell it. (Seneca)*

Qui desiderat pacem, praeparet bellum - *Let him who wishes for peace prepare for war. (Vegetius)*

Qui docet discit - *He who teaches learns*

Qui dormit, non peccat - *One who sleeps doesn't sin*

Qui habet aures audiendi audiat - *He who has ears, let him understand how to listen*

Qui ignorabat, ignorabitur - *One who is ignorant will remain unnoticed*

Qui me amat, amet et canem meum - *Love me, love my dog*

Qui multum habet, plus cupit - *He who has much desires more. (Seneca)*

Qui nimium probat, nihil probat - *One who proves too much, proves nothing*

Qui non est hodie cras minus aptus erit - *He who is not prepared today will be less so tomorrow. (Ovid)*

Qui omnes insidias timet in nullas incidit - *He who fears every ambush falls into none. (Pubilius Syrus)*

Qui potest capere capiat - *Let him accept it who can. Freely: If the shoe fits, wear it*

Qui pro innocente dicit, satis est eloquens - *He who speaks for the innocent is eloquent enough. (Publius Syrus)*

Qui scribit bis legit - *He who writes reads twice*

Qui tacet consentire videtur - *He that is silent is thought to consent*

Qui tacet consentit - *Silence gives consent*

Qui vir odiosus! - *What a bore!*

Qui vivat atque floreat ad plurimos annos - *May he live and flourish for many years*

Qui vult dare parva non debet magna rogare - *He who wishes to give little shouldn't ask for much*

Quia natura mutari non potest idcirco verae amicitiae sempiternae sunt - *Since nature cannot change, true friendships are eternal. (Horace)*

Quid agis, medice? - *What's up, Doc?*

Quid est illa in auqua? - *What's that in the water?*

Quid Novi - *What's New?*

Quid nunc - *What now?! (a nosy busybody)*

Quid pro quo - *Something for something. i.e. A favor for a favor*

Quid quid latine dictum sit, altum videtur - *Anything said in Latin sounds profound*

Quid rides? Mutato nomine de te fabula narratur - *What are you laughing at? Just change the name and the joke's on you. (Horace)*

Quidnunc? Or Quid nunc? - *What now? As a noun, a quidnunc is a busybody or a gossip*

Quidquid agis, prudenter agas et respice finem! - *Whatever you do, do cautiously, and look to the end*

Quidquid id est, timeo Danaos et dona ferentes - *Whatever it is, I fear the Greeks, even bearing gifts. (Vergil)*

Quidquid latine dictum sit, altum videtur - *Anything said in Latin sounds profound*

Quidvis Recte Factum Quamvis Humile Praeclarum - *Whatever is rightly done, however humble, is noble*

Quieta non movere - *Don't move settled things, or Don't rock the boat*

Quinon proficit deficit - *He who does not advance, go backwards*

Quique amavit, cras amet - *May he love tomorrow who has never loved before;*

Quis custodiet ipsos custodes - *Who shall keep watch over the guardians? (Luvenalis) Don't assign a fox to guard the henhouse*

Quis separabit? - *Who shall separate us?*

Quis, quid, ubi, quibus auxiliis, cur, quomodo, quando? - *Who, what, where, with what, why, how, when?*

Quisque comoedum est - *Everybody is a comedian*

Quo ad hoc - *As much as this (to this extent)*

Quo animo? - *With what spirit? (or intent?)*

Quo fas et gloria docunt - *Where right and glory lead*

Quo iure? - *By what law?*

Quo signo nata es? - *What's your sign?*

Quo usque tandem abutere, catilina, patientia nostra? - *How long will you abuse our patience, Catiline? (Cicero)*

Quo vadis? - *Where are you going? / Whither goest thou?*

Quod bonum, felix faustumque sit! - *May it be good, fortunate and prosperous! (Cicero)*

Quod differtur, non aufertur - *That which is postponed is not dropped. Inevitable is yet to happen. (Sir Thomas More)*

Quod erat demonstrandum (QED) - *Which was to be demonstrated*

Quod erat faciendum (QEF) - *Which was to be done*

Quod erat in veniendum - *Which was to be found*

Quod est (qe) - *Which is*

Quod foetet? - *What's that bad smell?*

Quod incepimus conficiemus - *What we have begun we shall finish*

Quod licet lovi non licet bovi - *What Jupiter (supreme God) is allowed to do, cattle (people) are not*

Quod minimum specimen in te ingenii? - *What microscopic evidence of wit can be found in you?*

Quod natura non sunt turpia - *What is natural*

cannot be bad

Quod vide (qv) - *See this thing*

Quomodo cogis comas tuas sic videri? - *How do you get your hair to do that?*

Quomodo vales - *How are you?*

Quorum - *Of whom*

Quos amor verus tenuit, tenebit - *True love will hold on to those whom it has held. (Seneca)*

Quot homines, tot sententiae - *As many men, so as many opinions*

Qvae nocent docent - *Things that hurt, teach. School of Hard Knocks*

Qvaerenda pecvnia primvm est, virtvs post nvmmos - *Money is the first thing to be sought [then] virtue after wealth*

Qvalis artifex pereo - *Such an artist dies in me - Emperor Nero's famous last words*

Qvalis pater talis filivs - *Like father like son. The apple doesn't fall too far from the tree*

Qvandoqve bonvs dormitat homervs - *Sometimes [even the] good Homer sleeps. You win some, you lose some*

Qvi bene amat bene castigat - *Who loves well castigates well. Spare the rod and spoil the child*

Qvi desiderat pacem praeparat bellvm - *Who desires peace [should] prepare [for] war*

Qvi docent discit - *He who teaches, learns. (George Bernard Shaw)*

Qvi fvgiebat rvrsvs proeliabitvr - *He who has fled will do battle once more. He who fights and runs away may live to fight another day*

Qvi me amat, amat et canem meam - *Who loves me loves my dog as well. Love me love my dog*

Qvi nescit dissimlare nescit regnare - *He who doesn't know how to lie doesn't know how to rule*

Qvid novi? - *What's new? 'What's up?'*

Qvod cibvs est aliis, aliis est wenenum - *What is food to some is poison to others. One man's meat is another poison*

Qvod cito acqviritvr cito perit - *[that] which is quickly acquired [is] quickly lost. Eeasy come, easy go*

Qvod erat demonstrandvm - *[that] which has been demonstrated - a statement of logical proof, especially in mathematics and law, abbreviated Q.E.D*

Qvod vive (q.v) - *Which see - a scholarly cross-reference*

R

Radicitus, comes! - *Really rad, dude!*

Radix lecti - *Couch potato*

Radix omnium malorum est cupiditas - *The love of money is the root of all evil. Avarice is the problem, money itself is not evil*

Raptus regaliter - *Royally screwed*

Rara avis - *A rare bird, i.e. An extraodinary or unusual thing. (Juvenal)*

Ratio decidendi - *The reason for the decision*

Ratio et consilium propriae ducis artes - *Reason and deliberation are the proper skills of a general*

Ratio legis est anima legis - *The reason of the law is the soul of the law*

Re vera, cara mea, mea nil refert - *Frankly my dear, I don't give a damn*

Re vera, potas bene - *Say, you sure are drinking a lot*

Re - *Concerning*

Recedite, plebes! Gero rem imperialem! - *Stand aside plebians! I am on imperial business!*

Recto - *On the right*

Redde Caesari quae sunt Caesaris - *Render unto Caesar the things that are Caesar's*

Redivivus - *Come back to life*

Redolet lvcernam - *[it] smells of the lamp - critical remark that one worked too hard on something*

Reductio ad absurdum - *Reduction to the absurd. (proving the truth of a proposition by proving the falsity of all its alternatives)*

Referendum - *Something to be referred*

Regina - *Queen*

Regnat non regitur qui nihil nisi quod vult facit - *He is a king and not a subject who does only what he wishes. (Syrus)*

Regnat populus - *Let the People rule*

Relata refero - *I tell what I have been told. (Herodotos)*

Religious loci - *The (religious) spirit of the place*

Rem tene, verba sequentur - *Keep to the subject and the words will follow. (Cato Senior)*

Repetitio est mater memoriae/ studiorum/ - *Repetition is the mother of memory/studies*

Requiescat in pace (RIP) - *May he/she rest in peace*

Rerum concordia discors - *The concord of things through discord. (Horace)*

Res firma mitescere nescit - *A firm resolve does not know how to weaken*

Res gestae - *Things done*

Res in cardine est - *The matter is on a door hinge*

things are balanced on a knife's edge

Res inter alios - *A matter between others it's not our busines*

Res ipsa loquitur - *The thing speaks for itself*

Res judicata - *Thing already judged upon*

Res melius evinissent cum coca - *Things go better with Coke*

Res publica - *The public thing*

Res severa est verum gaudium - *True joy is a serious thing. (Seneca)*

Res tantum valet quantum vendi potest - *A thing is worth only what someone else will pay for it*

Respice finem - *Look to the end*

Respice post te, mortalem te esse memento - *Look around you, remember that you are mortal. (Tertullianus)*

Respice, adspice, prospice - *Examine the past, examine the present, examine the future (look to the past, the present, the future)*

Respondeat superior - *Let the superior answer (a supervisor must take responsibility for the quality of a subordinate's work)*

Resurgam - *I shall rise again*

Revelare pecunia! - *Show me the money!*

Revera linguam latinam vix cognovi - *I dont really know all that much Latin*

Rex non potest peccare - *The king cannot sin*

Rex regnant sed non gubernat - *The king reigns but does not govern*

Rex - *King*

Rident stolidi verba latina - *Fools laugh at the Latin language. (Ovid)*

Ridentem dicere verum quid vetat? - *What forbids*

a laughing man from telling the truth? (Horace)
Rigor mortis - *The rigidity of death*
Risu inepto res ineptior nulla est - *There is nothing more foolish than a foolish laugh. (Catullus)*
Risus abundat in ore stultorum - *Abundant laughs in the mouth of the foolish - too much hilarity means foolishness*
Roma locuta est. Causa finita est - *Rome has spoken. The cause is finished*
Romani ite domum - *Romans go home!*
Romani quidem artem amatoriam invenerunt - *You know, the Romans invented the art of love*
Rosa rubicundior, lilio candidior, omnibus formosior, semper in te glorior - *Redder than the rose, whiter than the lilies, fairer than everything, I will always glory in thee*
Rumores volant. / Rumor volat - *Rumors fly. / Rumor flies*

S
Saepe creat molles aspera spina rosas - *Often the prickly thorn produces tender roses. (Ovid)*
Saepe ne utile quidem est scire quid futurum sit - *Often it is not even advantageous to know what will be. (Cicero)*
Saepe stilum vertas - *May you often turn the stylus (You should make frequent corrections.)*
Salus populi suprema lex - *The safety of the people is the supreme law. (Cicero)*
Salva veritate - *With truth preserved*
Salve (plural salvete) - *Hail; welcome*
Salve sis - *May you be well*
Salve veritate - *Saving the truth*
Salve(te) - *Greetings!*

Salve - *Hello*

Sanctum sanctorum - *The holy of holies*

Sane ego te vocavi. forsitan capedictum tuum desit - *I did call. Maybe your answering machine is broken*

Sapere aude! - *Dare to be wise! (Horace)*

Sapiens nihil affirmat quod non probat - *A wise man states as true nothing he does not prove (don't swear to anything you don't know firsthand)*

Sartor resartus - *The tailor patched*

Sat sapienti - *Enough for a wise man. (Plautus)*

Satis - *Enough*

Satius est impunitum relinqui facinus nocentis, quam innocentem damnari - *It is better that a crime is left unpunished than that an innocent man is punished. (Corpus Iuris Civilis)*

Scala Caeli - *The ladder of heaven*

Scala naturae - *The ladder of nature*

Scandalum magnatum - *Scandal of magnates*

Schola cantorum - *School of singers*

Scientia est potentia - *Knowledge is power*

Scientia non habet inimicum nisp ignorantem - *Science has no enemies but the ignorants*

Scilicet (sc.) - *That is to say*

Scio cur summae inter se dissentiant! Numeris Romanis utor! - *I know why the numbers don't agree! I use Roman numerals!*

Scio me nihil scire - *I know that I know nothing. Certain knowledge cannot be obtained. (Socrates)*

Scire tuum nihil est, nisi te scire hoc sciat alter - *Your knowledge is nothing when no one else knows that you know it*

Sciri facias - *Cause (him) to know*

Scito te ipsum - *Know yourself*
Scribere est agere - *To write is to act*
Scripsit - *He/she wrote it*
Sculpsit - *He/she engraved it*
Sed quis custodiet ipsos custodes? - *Who watches the watchmen? (Juvenal)*
Sedit qui timuit ne non succederet - *He who feared he would not succeed sat still. (For fear of failure, he did nothing.) (Horace)*
Semper fidelis - *Always faithful*
Semper idem - *Always the same thing. (Cicero)*
Semper inops quicumque cupit - *Whoever desires is always poor. (Claudian)*
Semper letteris mandate - *Always get it in writing!*
Semper paratus - *Always prepared*
Semper superne nitens - *Always striving upwards*
Semper ubi sub ubi ubique - *Always wear underwear everywhere*
Senatus Populusque Romanus (SPQR) - *The Senate and the Roman people*
Sensu lato - *Broadly speaking*
Sensu stricto - *Strictly speaking*
Sensu stricto, nullo metro compositum est - *Strictly speaking, it doesn't rhyme*
Sentio aliquos togatos contra me conspirare - *I think some people in togas are plotting against me*
Sequens (seq.) - *The following (one)*
Sequens mirabitur aetas - *The following age will be amazed*
Sequentia (seqq.) - *The following (ones)*
Seriatim - *One after another in order*
Serva me, servabo te - *Save me and I will save you. (Petronius Arbiter)*

Si Deus pro nobis quis contra nos - *If God is with us who is against us*

Si fallatis officium, quaestor infitias eat se quicquam scire de factis vestris - *If you fail, the secretary will disavow all knowledge of your activities*

Si fecisti nega! - *If you did it, deny it (stonewall!)*

Si finis bonus est, totum bonum erit - *If the end is good, everything will be good (all's well that ends well)*

Si fractum non sit, noli id reficere - *If it ain't broke, don't fix it*

Si hoc legere scis nimium eruditionis habes - *Essentially it says, 'if you can read this, you're overeducated.'*

Si hoc non legere potes tu asinus es - *If you can't read this, you're an ass*

Si minor plus est ergo nihil sunt omnia - *If less is more, then nothing is everything*

Si monumentum requiris circumspice - *If you seek a monument, look around*

Si post fata venit gloria non propero - *If glory comes after death, I'm not in a hurry (if one must die to be recognised, I can wait)*

Si sapis, sis apis - *If you are wise, be a bee*

Si tacuisses, philosophus manisses - *If you had kept quiet, you would have remained a philosopher. (Boethius)*

Si tu id aeficas, ei venient. Ager somnia - *If you build it, they will come*

Si vis amari, ama - *If you wish to be loved, love. (Seneca)*

Si vis pacem, para bellum - *If you want peace,*

prepare for the war. (Vegetius)

Sic ad nauseam - *And so on to the point of causing nausea*

Sic erat in fatis - *So it was fated*

Sic faciunt omnes - *Everyone is doing it*

Sic friatur crustum dulce - *That's the way the cookie crumbles*

Sic itur ad astra - *Such is the path to the stars (i.e. Gain reputation) (Vergil)*

Sic passim - *Thus everywhere*

Sic semper tyrannis - *Thus always to tyrants - a statement often accompanying a regicide*

Sic transit gloria mundi - *So passes the glory of the world*

Sic volo, sic iubeo - *I want this, I order this. (Juvenalis)*

Sic - *Thus, just so*

Silent enim leges inter arma - *Laws are silent in times of war. (Cicero)*

Simia quam similis, turpissimus bestia, nobis! - *How like us is that very ugly beast the monkey. (Cicero)*

Simplex munditiis - *Unaffected by manners. (Horace)*

Simpliciter - *Naturally; without qualification*

Sine cura - *Without a care*

Sine die - *Without a day (indefinitely)*

Sine ira et studio - *Without anger or bias. (Tacitus)*

Sine loco (sl) - *Without place*

Sine nobilitatis - *Without nobility (SNOB)*

Sine prole (sp) - *Without issue*

Sine qua non - *Something/someone indispensable*

Sine sole sileo - *Without the sun I'm silent. (sundial* *inscription)*

Siste, viator - *Wait, traveler - inscription on Roman tombstones*

Sit tibi terra levis - *May the earth be light upon you - tombstone inscription*

Sit vis vobiscum - *May the Force be with you. (Star Wars)*

Sobria inebrietas - *Sober intoxication*

Sol omnibus lucet - *The sun shines upon us all. (Petronius)*

Sola lingua bona est lingua mortua - *The only good language is a dead language*

Solitudinem fecerunt, pacem appelunt - *They made a desert and called it peace. (Tacitus)*

Solum potestis prohibere ignes silvarum - *Only you are can prevent forest fires*

Sona si latine loqueris - *Honk if you speak Latin*

Sotto voce - *In soft voice*

Spectaculorum procedere debet - *The show must go on*

Spectatvm venivnt, venivnt spectentvr vt ipsae - *They come to see, they come that they themselves be seen 'to see and be seen*

Spemque metumque inter dubiis - *Hover between hope and fear. (Vergil)*

Spero melior - *I hope for better things*

Spero nos familiares mansuros - *I hope we'll still be friends*

Spiritus asper - *Rough breathing*

Spiritus lenis - *Smooth breathing*

Splendide mendax - *Splendidly false. (Horace)*

Splendor sine occasu - *Splendour without end*

Stabat Mater - *The mother was standing*

Stare decisis - *To stand by things decided*
Status quo - *The current state of being*
Stercus accidit - *Shit happens*
Stet - *Let it stand*
Struit insidias lacrimis cum femina plorat - *When a woman weeps, she is setting traps with her tears. (Dionysius Cato)*
Studium discendi voluntate quae cogi non potest constat - *Study depends on the good will of the student, a quality which cannot be secured by compulsion*
Stultior stulto fuisti, qui tabellis crederes! - *Idiot of idiots, to trust what is written!*
Stultorum calami carbones moenia chartae - *Chalk is the pen of fools, walls (their) paper No Graffiti please. Showing that graffiti is nothing new*
Stultorum infinitus est numerus - *Infinite is the number of fools. (Bible)*
Stultum est timere quod vitare non potes - *It is foolish to fear that which you cannot avoid. (Publilius Syrus)*
Stultus est sicut stultus facit - *Stupid is as stupid does*
Sua cuique voluptas - *Everyone has his own pleasures*
Sub dio - *Under the open sky*
Sub iudice - *Under a judge*
Sub judice - *Before a court*
Sub lite - *In dispute*
Sub poena - *Under penalty of law*
Sub rosa - *Under the rose. Secretly or in confidence*
Sub secreto - *In secret*

Sub silentio - *In silence*
Sub sole nihil novi est - *There's nothing new under the sun*
Sub voce (sv) - *Under the voice*
Subucula tua apparet - *Your slip is showing*
Suggestio falsi - *Suggestion of something false*
Suggestio veri, suggestio falsi - *An intimation of truth, an intimation of falcity*
Sui generis - *Of his/her/its kind*
Sui iuris - *Of one's own right*
Sum, ergo edo - *I am, therefore I eat*
Summa cum laude - *With highest honor*
Summam scrutemur - *Let's look at the bottom line*
Summum bonum - *The highest good*
Summum ius, summa iniuria - *The extreme law is the greatest injustice. (Cicero)*
Sumptus censum ne superet - *Let not your spending exceed your income (live within your means)*
Sunt lacrimae rerum et mentem mortalia tangunt - *These are the tears of things, and our mortality cuts to the heart. (Vergil)*
Sunt pueri pueri, puerilia tractant - *Children are children, (therefore) children do childish things*
Suntne vacci laeti - *Are your cows happy?*
Suo iure - *In one's own right*
Suo jure - *In one's rightful place*
Suos cuique mos - *Everyone has his customs. (Gellius)*
Supra - *Above or on an earlier page*
Sursum corda - *Lift up your hearts (to God)*
Suum cuique pulchrum est - *To each his own is*

beautiful. *(Cicero)*

Svi generis - *Of its own kind unique*

T

Tabula rasa - *A clean slate. Person that knows nothing*

Tacet - *Silence*

Tam diu minime visu! - *Long time, no see!*

Tam exanimis quam tunica nehru fio - *I am as dead as the nehru jacket*

Tamdiu discendum est, quamdiu vivas - *We should learn as long as we may live. (We live and learn.) (Seneca Philosophus)*

Tamquam alter idem - *As if a second self. (Cicero)*

Tanta stultitia mortalium est - *What fools these mortals be*

Tantum eruditi sunt liberi - *Only the educated are free. (Epictetus)*

Tantum religio potuit suadere malorum - *So potent was religion in persuading to evil deeds. (Lucretius)*

Tarditas et procrastinatio odiosa est - *Delay and procrastination is hateful. (Cicero)*

Te audire non possum. Musa sapientum fixa est in aure - *I can't hear you. I have a banana in my ear*

Te capiam, cunicule sceleste! - *I'll get you, you wascally wabbit!*

Te Deum - *Thee, God [we praise]*

Te igitur - *Thee, therefore*

Te nosce - *Know thyself*

Te precor dulcissime supplex! - *Pretty please with a cherry on top!*

Tempora mutantur, nos et mutamur in illis - *The times change, and we change with them. (John*

Owen)

Tempore - *In the time of*

Tempus edax rerum - *Time is the devourer of things (time flies)*

Tempus fugit, non autem memoria - *Time flies, but not memory*

Tempus fugit - *Time flees*

Tempus incognitum - *Time unknown*

Tempus neminem manet - *Time waits for no one*

Tempus omnia sed memorias privat - *Time deprives all but memories*

Ter in die (t.i.d.) - *Three times a day*

Terminus a quo - *The end from which*

Terminus ad quem - *The end to which*

Terra firma - *Solid ground*

Terra incognita - *Unknown land*

Terra nullius - *Uninhabited land*

Tertium quid - *A third something*

Tetigisti acu - *You have hit the nail on the head. (Plautus)*

Theatrum mundi - *The theatre of the world*

Tibi gratias agimus quod nihil fumas - *Thank you for not smoking*

Timendi causa est nescire - *Ignorance is the cause of fear. (Seneca)*

Timeo Danaos et dona ferentes - *I fear the Greeks, even when they bring gifts. (Virgil)*

Timor mortis conturbat me - *The fear of death confounds me*

Tintinnuntius meus sonat! - *There goes my beeper!*

Tolerabiles ineptiae - *Bearable absurdities*

Totidem verbis - *In so many words*

Totum dependeat! - *Let it all hang out!*

Trahimur omnes laudis studio - *We are all led on by our eagerness for praise. (Cicero)*

Transire suum pectus mundoque potiri - *To overcome one's human limitations and become master of the universe*

Transit umbra, lux permanet - *Shadow passes, light remains (On a sun dial)*

Tu autem - *You, also*

Tu fui, ego eris - *What you are, I was. What I am, you will be. (This is found on graves and burial sites)*

Tu ne cede malis sed contra audentior ito - *Yield not to misfortunes, but advance all the more boldly against them*

Tu quoque Brute, file mi! - *You too Bruto, my son! (Caesar's last words)*

Tu quoque - *You likewise*

Tu stupidus es - *You are dumb*

Tu, rattus turpis! - *You dirty rat!*

Tua mater tam antiquior ut linguam latine loquatur - *Your mother is so old she speaks Latin*

Tua toga suspina est - *Your toga is backwards*

Tuis pugis pignore! - *You bet your bippy!*

Tum podem extulit horridulum - *You are talking shit*

U

Uberrimae fidei - *Of the utmost good faith*

Ubi amor, ibi oculus - *Where love is, there is insight*

Ubi bene, ibi patria - *Where you feel good, there is your home*

Ubi concordia, ibi victoria - *Where is the unity,*

there is the victory. (Publius Syrus)
Ubi dubium ibi libertas - *Where there is doubt, there is freedom*
Ubi est mea anaticula cumminosa? - *Wheres my rubber ducky?*
Ubi fumus, ibi ignis - *Where there's smoke, there's fire*
Ubi maior, minor cessat - *The weak (minor) capitulates before the strong (major)*
Ubi mel ibi apes - *Where honey, there bees, i.e., if you want support, you must offer something in return*
Ubi revera (Ubi re vera) - *When, in reality*
Ubi spiritus est cantus est - *Where there is spirit there is song*
Ubi sunt? - *Where are they (the good old days)?*
Ubi supra - *Where (cited) above*
Ubicumque homo est, ibi benefici locus est - *Wherever there is a man, there is a place of/for kindness/service*
Ubique - *Everywhere*
Ultima ratio regum - *The final argument of kings*
Ultima ratio - *Ultimate sanction*
Ultima Thule - *The most distant Thule*
Ultimo (ult.) - *Of the previous month*
Ultimus Romanorum - *The last of the Romans*
Ultra posse nemo obligatur - *No one is obligated beyond what he is able to do*
Ultra vires - *Beyond the powers or legal authority*
Un idea perplexi na - *The idea is strange to us*
Una hirundo non facit ver - *One Swallow does not make Summer. (Horace)*
Una salus victis nullam sperare salutem - *The*

one safety for the vanquished is to abandon hope of safety knowing there is no hope can give one the courage to fight and win

Una voce - *With one's voice*

Unitam logica falsa tuam philosophiam totam suffodiant! - *May faulty logic undermine your entire philosophy!*

Unitas mirabile vinculum - *The wonderful bond of unity*

Unum necessarium - *The one necessary*

Unus multorum - *One of many. (Horace)*

Urbanus et instructus - *A gentleman and a scholar*

Urbem lateritiam invenit, marmoream reliquit - *He found a city [Rome] of bricks and left a city of marble. (Augustus)*

Urbi et orbi - *To the city [Rome] and to the globe - a blessing of the pope*

Ut ameris, ama! - *To be loved, love!*

Ut desint vires, tamen est laudanda voluntas - *Although the power is lacking, the will is commendable. (Ovid)*

Ut dictum (ut dict.) - *As directed*

Ut humiliter opinor - *In my humble opinion*

Ut incepit fidelis sic permanet - *As loyal as she began, so she remains*

Ut infra - *As below*

Ut sementem feceris, ita metes - *As you sow, so shall you reap. (Cicero)*

Ut si! - *As if!*

Ut sit magna, tamen certe lenta ira deorum est - *The wrath of the gods may be great, but it certainly is slow*

Ut supra (ut sup.) - *As above*

Uti foro - *To play the market*
Uti possidetis - *As you possess*
Uti, non abuti - *To use, not abuse*
Utile et dulce - *Useful and pleasant*
Utinam barbari spatium proprium tuum invadant! - *May barbarians invade your personal space!*
Utinam coniurati te in foro interficiant! - *May conspirators assassinate you in the mall!*
Utinam populus romanus unam cervicem haberet! - *If only the Roman people had one neck!*
Uva uvam videndo varia fit - *A grape changes color in seeing another grape. A bad/good friend makes you a bad/good person*

V

Vacca foeda - *Stupid cow*
Vacca, vacca, vacca - *Cow, cow, cow*
Vade in pace - *Go in peace. (Roman way of saying goodbye)*
Vade mecum - *Come with me. A constant companion*
Vae victis! - *Woe to the conquered! (vanquished) (Livy)*
Vagans - *Cruising*
Vah! Denuone Latine loquebar? Me ineptum. Interdum modo elabitur - *Oh! Was I speaking Latin again? Silly me. Sometimes it just sort of slips out*
Vale, lacerte! - *See you later, alligator!*
Vale - *Farewell*
Valui ad satanam in computatrum meum invocandum - *I succeeded in summoning satan into my computer*

Vanitas vanitatvm, omnis vanitas - *Vanity of vanities, all is vanity*

Varia lecto (v.l.) - *Variant reading*

Variatio delectat - *There's nothing like change! (Cicero)*

Variorum - *Of various people*

Velle est posse - *To be willing is to be able*

Veni vidi duci - *I came, I saw, I calculated*

Veni, vidi, vici - *I came, I saw, I conquered. (Julius Caesar)*

Veni, Vidi, Visa - *I Came, I Saw, I Shopped*

Veni, Vidi, volo in domum redire - *I came, I saw, I want to go home*

Venienti occurrite morbo - *Meet the misfortune as it comes. (Persius)*

Venire facias - *You must make come*

Ventis secundis, tene cursum - *Go with the flow*

Ventis secundis, tene/tenete cursum - *The winds being favorable, hold the course*

Verba de futuro - *Words about the future*

Verba movent, exempla trahunt - *Words move people, examples draw/compel them. Deeds, not words, give the example*

Verba volant, (littera) scripta manet - *Words fly away, the written (letter) remains*

Verbatim et litteratim - *Word for word and letter for letter*

Verbatim - *Exactly as said*

Verbum sapienti satis est (verb. sap.) - *A word to the wise is sufficient. Enough said*

Veritas Lux Mea - *The truth enlightens me / The truth is my light*

Veritas numquam perit - *Truth never perishes.*

(Seneca)

Veritas odit moras - *Truth hates delay. (Seneca)*

Veritas vincit - *Truth conquers*

Veritas vos liberabit - *The truth will set you free*

Verso - *Reverse*

Versus - *Against*

Verum et factum convertuntur - *The true and the made are interchangeable. One can know with certainty only what he have created himself*

Verveces tui similes pro ientaculo mihi appositi sunt - *I have jerks like you for breakfast*

Vesanum poetam qui sapiunt fugiunt - *Anyone with a brain flees a versifying poet*

Vescere bracis meis - *Eat my shorts*

Vestigia terrent - *The footprints frighten me. (Horace)*

Vestis virum reddit - *The clothes make the man. (Quintilianus)*

Veto - *I forbid*

Vi et armis - *By force and arms*

Via Crucis - *The Way of the Cross*

Via Dolorosa - *The Way of Sorrow*

Via Lactea - *The Milky Way*

Via media - *A middle way or course*

Via - *By way of*

Vice versa - *In reverse order*

Vice - *In place of*

Victis honor - *Honour to the vanquished*

Victoria Imperatrix Regina (VIR) - *Victoria, Empress and Queen*

Victoria Regina (VR) - *Queen Victoria*

Victoria Regina et Imperatrix (VRI) - *Victoria, Queen and Empress*

Victoria, non praeda - *Victory, not loot*

Victurus te saluto - *He who is about to win salutes you*

Vide et credere - *See and believe*

Vide ut supra - *See the above*

Vide - *See*

Videlicet (viz.) - *That is to say; To wit; Namely*

Video meliora proboque deteriora sequor - *I see the better way and approve it, but I follow the worse way*

Videre est credere - *Seeing is believing*

Videtis quantum scelus contra rem publicam vobis nuntiatum sit? - *How great an evil do you see that may have been announced by you against the Republic? (Cicero)*

Vidistine nuper imagines moventes bonas? - *Seen any good movies lately?*

Vigilando, agendo, bene consulendo, prospera omnia cedunt - *By watching, by doing, by counsulting well, these things yield all things prosperous. (Sallust)*

Vincere est totum - *To win is everything*

Vincit omnia amor - *Love conquers all*

Vincit omnia veritas - *Truth conquers all*

Vincit qui se vincit - *He conquers who conquers himself*

Vinculum unitatis - *The bond of unity*

Vinum bellum iucunumque est, sed animo corporeque caret - *It's a nice little wine, but it lacks character and depth*

Vinum et musica laetificant cor - *Wine and music gladden the heart*

Vir bonus, dicendi peritus - *A good man, skilled in*

speaking. (definition of an orator) (Cato the Elder)

Vir prudens non contra ventum mingit - *A wise man does not urinate against the wind*

Vir sapit qui pauca loquitor - *It is a wise man who speaks little*

Vir sapit qui pauca loquitur - *That man is wise who talks little (know when to hold your tongue)*

Vires acquirit eundo - *It gains strength by going / as it goes. (Virgil)*

Virginibus puerisque - *For maidens and youths*

Virgo intacta - *Intact virgin*

Viri sunt viri - *Men are slime*

Virtus in medio stat - *Virtue stands in the middle*

Virtute et armis - *By courage and by arms*

Virtvs probata florescit - *Manly excellence in trial flourished*

Virtvtis fortvna comes - *Good luck is the companion of courage*

Virum mihi, Camena, insece versutum - *Tell me, O Muse, of the skillful man. (Livius Andronicus)*

Virus - *Poison or slime*

Vis comica - *Sense of humour*

Vis consili expers mole ruit sua - *Brute force bereft of wisdom falls to ruin by its own weight. (Discretion is the better part of valor) (Horace)*

Vis inertiae - *The power of inertia - why things never change*

Vis maior - *Higher force*

Vis medicatrix naturae - *The healing power of nature*

Visa - *Things seen*

Visne saltare? Viam Latam Fungosam scio - *Do you want to dance? I know the Funky Broadway*

Visne saltare? - *Do you want to dance?*
Vita brevis, ars lunga - *Life is short, art is long*
Vita contin git. Vive com eo - *Life happens. Live with it*
Vita luna! - *Crazy life!*
Vita mutatur, non tollitur - *Life is changed, not taken away*
Vita non est vivere sed valere vita est - *Life is more than merely staying alive*
Vita sine libris mors est - *Life without books is death*
Vitam impendere vero - *To risk one's life for the truth*
Vitam regit fortuna, non sapientia - *Fortune, not wisdom, rules lives. (Cicero)*
Vitanda est improba siren desidia - *One must avoid that wicked temptress, Laziness. (Horace)*
Vitiis nemo sine nascitur - *No-one is born without faults. (Horace)*
Viva voce - *With living voice*
Vivat regina - *Long live the queen*
Vivat rex - *Long live the king*
Vivat, crescat, floreat! - *May he/she/it live, grow, and flourish!*
Vive hodie - *Live today (not tomorrow)*
Vive vt vivas - *Live that you may live*
Vivere commune est, sed non commune mereri - *Everybody lives; not everybody deserves to*
Vivere disce, cogita mori - *Learn to live; Remember death. (sundial inscription)*
Vivos voco, mortuos plango - *I call the living, I mourn the dead. (church bell inscription)*
Vix ulla tam iniqua pax, quin bello vel

aequissimo sit potior - *Scarcely is there any peace so unjust that it is better than even the fairest war. (Erasmus)*

Vixere fortes ante agamemnona - *Brave men lived before Agamemnon. (heroism exists even if it's not recorded)*

Vixit - *He/she has lived*

Vltima ratio regvm - *The final argument of kings. (motto of Louis XIV on his cannon)*

Vltra vires - *Beyond [one's] authority outside the jurisdiction*

Volens et potens - *Willing and able*

Volente Deo - *God willing*

Volenti non fit iniuria - *A person who consents does not suffer injustice*

Volo anaticulam cumminosam meam! - *I want my rubber ducky!*

Volo, non valeo - *I am willing but unable*

Volvptates commendat rarior vsvs - *Infrequent use commends pleasure. (moderation in all things)*

Vos vestros servate, meos mihi linquite mores - *You cling to your own ways and leave mine to me. (Petrarch)*

Vox clamantis in deserto - *Voice crying in the desert. (voice in the wilderness unheeded warning, an opinion not in the mainstream*

Vox populi, vox Dei - *The voice of the people is the voice of God. (Public opinion is obligatory)*

Vox populi - *The voice of the people*

Vrbi et orbi - *To the city and to the world. (preface of Papal documents)*

Vulnerant omnes, ultima necat - *Every (hour) wounds, the last kills. (sundial inscription)*

Vulpem pilum mutat, non mores - *A fox may change its hair, not its tricks. (People change behaviour but not their aims)*
Vultus est index animi - *The face is the index of the soul/mind*

SOME LATIN MOTTOES (or TAGS/ABBREVIATIONS)

Time reveals the truth.	Veritatem dies aperit.
No one deserves punishment for a thought.	Cogitationis poenam nemo meretur.
Know thyself.	Nosce te ipsum.
False in one thing, false in everything.	Falsus in uno, falsus in omnibus.
Nothing is swifter than rumor.	Fama nihil est celerius.
Wise is the person who talks little.	Vir sapit qui pauca loquitur.
Where there is smoke, there is fire.	Flamma fumo est proxima.
Inconvenience does not serve as an argument.	Incommodum non servit argumentum.
Silence speaks louder than words.	Cum tacent, clamant.
A word is enough for a wise man.	Verbum sat sapienti.

After the battle, the reward.	Post proelium, praemium.
After this, therefore because of this.	Post hoc, ergo propter hoc.
As in painting, so in poetry.	Ut pictura poesis.
Better late than never.	Potius sero quam numquam.
Beware of the dog.	Cave canem.
A sound mind in a healthy body.	Mens sana in corpore sano.
Birds of a feather flock together.	Pares cum paribus facillime congregantur.
Death is the final accounting.	Mors ultima ratio.
Divide and rule.	Divide et impera.
Eternal vigilance is the price of liberty.	Vigilia pretium libertatis.
A.D.	*anno Domini* - in the year of the Lord
a.m.	*ante meridiem* - before noon
cf.	*confer* – compare
d.v.	*deus volens - god*

	willing
e.g.	*exempli gratia* - for example
et al.	*et alii* - and others
etc.	*et cetera* - and so forth
ibid.	*ibidem* - in the same place
id.	*idem* - the same (author)
i.e.	*id est* - that is
N.B.	*nota bene* - note well
op. cit.	*opere citato* - in the volume quoted
p.m.	*post meridiem* - after noon
pro tem.	*pro tempore* - for the time being
P.S.	*post scriptum* - written afterwards
q.v.	*quod vide* - which see
vs.	*versus* - against
First come, first served.	Potior est, qui prior est.

For the public good.	Pro bono publico.
Forewarned, forearmed.	Praemonitus, praemunitus.
Fortune favors the brave.	Audentes fortuna iuvat.
Go in peace.	Vade in pace
Grasp the subject, the words will follow.	Rem tene; verba sequentur.
He conquers who conquers himself.	Vincit, qui se vincit.
He gives twice, who gives promptly.	Bis dat qui cito dat.
He who does not advance, goes backward.	Qui non proficit deficit.
He who is silent consents.	Qui tacet consentit.
He whom the gods love dies young.	Quem di diliqunt adolescens moritur.
I came, I saw, I conquered.	Veni, vidi, vici.
I have liberated my soul.	Liberavi animam meam.
If you wish for peace, prepare for war.	Si vis pacem, para bellum.
In wine is truth.	In vino veritas.

It is sweet and honorable to die for one's country.	Dulce et decorum est pro patria mori.
Know thyself.	Nosce te ipsum.
Leisure without literature is death.	Otium sine litteris mors est.
Let no one be willing to speak ill of the absent.	Absenti nemo non nocuisse velit.
Let the buyer beware.	Caveat emptor.
Leisure with dignity.	Otium cum dignitate.
Live that you may live.	Vive ut vivas.
Love conquers all things; let us too surrender to love.	Omnia vincit amor; et nos cedamus amori.
May he rest in peace.	Requiescat in pace (RIP).
Moderation in all things.	Ne quid nimis.
Necessity is the mother of invention.	Mater artium necessitas.
Never despair.	Nil desperandum.
No one provokes me with impunity.	Nemo me impune lacessit.
Not for self, but for all.	Non sibi, sed omnibus.
Not quantity but quality (not	Non multa sed multum.

many but much).

Nothing can be created from nothing.	Nil posse creari de nilo.
Nothing in excess.	Nihil [or Ne quid] nimis.
Peace be with you.	Pax vobiscum.
Practise yourself what you preach.	Facias ipse quod faciamus suades.
Red-handed.	Flagrante delicto.
Seize the day.	Carpe diem.
So passes away earthly glory.	Sic transit gloria mundi.
The cowl does not make a monk.	Cucullus non facit monachum.
The die is cast.	Iacta alea est.
The first among equals.	Primus inter pares.
The poet is born, not made.	Poeta nascitur, non fit.
The times change and we change with them.	Tempora mutantur, nos et mutamur in illis.
Time flies.	Tempus fugit.
To err is human.	Errare humanum est.
To the city and to the world.	Urbi et orbi.

Truth conquers all things.	Vincit omnia veritas.	
With you I should love to live, with you be ready to die.	Tecum vivere amem, tecum obeam libens.	
Woe to the conquered!	Vae victis!	
You sow for yourself, you reap for yourself.	Tibi seris, tibi metis.	
To pray is to work, to work is to pray.	Orare est laborare, laborare est orare.	Benedictine Monks
To the greater glory of God.	Ad maiorem Dei gloriam.	Jesuit Order
May knowledge increase.	Crescat scientia.	University of Chicago
Light and truth.	Lux et veritas.	Yale University
The truth shall make you free.	Veritas vos liberabit.	John Hopkins University
Always faithful.	Semper fidelis.	U.S. Marine Corps
Always	Semper	U.S. Coast

prepared.	paratus.	Guards
Justice to all.	Justitia omnibus.	District of Columbia (USA Capital)
Out of many, one.	E pluribus unum.	United States
No one wounds me with impunity.	Nemo me impune lacessit.	Scotland
Labour conquers all things.	Labor omnia vincit.	Oklahoma

101 different ways of saying 'I love you'

The English dictionary describes love as deep, tender, ineffable feeling of affection and solicitude toward a person, such as that arising from kinship, recognition of attractive qualities, or a sense of underlying oneness. Here 'I love you' as defined in relationships between people, with translations from many different languages and dialects.

1. Afrikaans - Ek is lief vir jou

2. Albanian - te dua

3. Alentejano (Portugal) - Gosto De Ti, Porra!

4. Alsacien (Elsass) - Ich hoan dich gear

5. Amharic (Aethio.) - Afekrishalehou

6. Arabic - Ana Ahebak / Ana Bahibak

7. Armenian - yes kez shat em siroom

8. Assamese - Moi tomak bhal pau

9. Assyr - Az tha hijthmekem

10. Bahasa Malayu (Malaysia) - Saya cinta mu

11. Bambara - M'bi fe

12. Bangla - Ami tomakay bala basi

13. Bangladeschi - Ami tomake walobashi

14. Basque - Nere maitea

15. Batak - Holong rohangku di ho

16. Bavarian - tuI mog di

17. Belarusian - Ya tabe kahayu

18. Bengali - Ami tomake bhalobashi

19. Berber - Lakh tirikh

20. Bicol - Namumutan ta ka

21. Bisaya - Nahigugma ako kanimo

22. Bolivian Quechua - Qanta munani

23. Bosnian - Ja te volim (formally) or volim-te
Turkish seni seviyorum

24. Bulgarian - As te obicham

25. Bulgarian - Obicham te

26. Burmese - chit pa de

27. Cambodian (to the female) - bon saleng oun

28. Cambodian (to the male) - oun saleng bon

29. Canadian French - Je t'adore ("I love you")

30. Canadian French - Je t'aime ("I like you")

31. Catalan - T'estim (mallorcan)

32. Cebuano - Gihigugma ko ikaw

33. Chamoru (or Chamorro) - Hu guaiya hao

34. Cherokee - Tsi ge yu i

35. Cheyenne - Ne mohotatse

36. Chichewa - Ndimakukonda

37. Chickasaw - Chiholloli (first 'i' nasalized)

38. Chinese - Ngo oi ney a (Cantonese)

39. Chinese - Wuo ai nee (Mandarin)

40. Corsican - Ti tengu cara (to female)

41. Corsican - Ti tengu caru (to male)

42. Creol - Mi aime jou

43. Croatian - Volim te (used in common speech)

44. Czech - Miluji Te

45. Danish - Jeg elsker dig

46. Dutch - Ik hou van jou

47. Dutch - Jeg elsker dig

48. Ecuador Quechua - Canda munani

49. English - I love thee (used only in Christian context)

50. English - I love you

51. Eskimo - Nagligivaget

52. Esperanto - Mi amas vim

53. Estonian - Ma armastan sind / Mina armastan sind (formal)

54. Ethiopia - afekereshe alhu

55. Faroese - Eg elski teg

56. Farsi - Tora dost daram

57. Filipino - Mahal ka ta

58. Finnish (Minä) rakastan sinua

59. Flemish (Ghent) - 'k'ou van ui

60. French (formal) - Je vous aime

61. Friesian - Ik hald fan dei

62. Gaelic - Tá mé i ngrá leat

63. Galician - Querote (or) Amote

64. Georgian - Miquar shen

65. German - Ich liebe Dich

66. Ghanaian - Me dor wo

67. Greek - agapo se

68. Greek - S'agapo

69. Greenlandic - Asavakit

70. Gronings - Ik hol van die

71. Gujarati - oo tane prem karu chu

72. Hausa - Ina sonki

73. Hawaiian - Aloha au ia`oe

74. Hebrew - Ani ohevet ota

75. Hiligaynon - Guina higugma ko ikaw

76. Hindi - Main tumsey pyaar karta hoon / Maine Pyar Kiya

77. Hmong - Kuv hlub koj

78. Hokkien - Wa ai lu

79. Hopi - Nu' umi unangwa'ta

80. Hungarian - Szeretlek te'ged

81. Icelandic - Eg elska thig

82. Ilocano - Ay ayating ka

83. Indi - Mai Tujhe Pyaar Kartha Ho

84. Indonesian - Saya cinta padamu ('Saya', commonly used)

85. Inuit - Negligevapse

86. Iranian - Mahn doostaht doh-rahm

87. Irish - taim i' ngra leat

88. Italian - Ti amo/Ti voglio bene

89. Japanese - Anata wa, dai suki desu

90. Javanese (formal) - Kulo tresno marang panjenengan

91. Javanese (informal) - aku terno kowe

92. Kannada - Naanu ninna preetisuttene

93. Kapampangan - Kaluguran daka

94. Kenya (Kalenjin) - Achamin

95. Kenya (Kiswahili) - Ninakupenda

96. Kikongo - Mono ke zola nge (mono ke' zola nge')

97. Kiswahili - Nakupenda

98. Konkani - Tu magel moga cho

99. Korean - SA LANG HAE / Na No Sa Lan Hei

100. Kurdish - Khoshtm Auyt

101. Laos - Chanrackkun

102. Latin - Te amo

103. Latvian - Es mîlu Tevi

104. Lebanese - Bahibak

105. Lingala - Nalingi yo

106. Lithuanian - As Myliu Tave

107. Lojban - mi do prami

108. Luo - Aheri

109. Luxembourgeois - Ech hun dech gäer

110. Macedonian - Jas Te Sakam

111. Madrid - lingo Me molas, tronca

112. Maiese - Wa wa

113. Malay - Saya cintakan mu / Saya cinta mu

114. Maltese - Inhobbok hafna

115. Marathi - Me tula prem karto

116. Mohawk - Kanbhik

117. Moroccan - Ana moajaba bik

118. Nahuatl - Ni mits neki

119.   Navaho - Ayor anosh'ni

120.   Ndebele - Niyakutanda

121.   Nigeria (Hausa) - Ina sonki

122.   Nigeria (Yoruba langauge) - Mo fe ran re

123.   Norwegian - Jeg elsker deg

124.   Osetian - Aez dae warzyn

125.   Pakistan (Urdu) - May tum say pyar karta hun

126.   Pandacan - Syota na kita!!

127.   Pangasinan - Inaru Taka

128.   Papiamento - Mi ta stimabo

129.   Persian - Tora Doost Darem

130.   Pig Latin - I-yea Ove-lea Ou-yea

131.   Polish - Kocham Cie

132.   Portuguese (Brazilian) - Eu te amo

133.   Punjabi - me tumse pyar ker ta hu'

134.   Quenya - Tye-mela'ne

135.   Romanian - Te ador (stronger)

136.   Romanian - Te iubesc

137.   Russian - Ya tyebya lyublyu

138.   Samoan - Ou te alofa outou

139.   Sanskrit - tvayi snihyaami

140.   Scottish Gaelic - Tha gra\dh agam ort

141.   Serbo-Croatian - Volim te

142. Setswana - Ke a go rata

143. Shona - Ndinokuda

144. Sindhi - Maa tokhe pyar kendo ahyan

145. Singhalese - Mama oyaata aadareyi

146. Slovenian - ljubim te

147. South Sotho - Ke o Rata

148. Spanish - Te quiero / te amo / yo amor

149. Sri Lanka - mame adhare

150. Surinam - Mi lobi joe

151. Swahili - Naku penda

152. Swedish - Jag älskar dig

153. Swiss-German - Ch-ha di gärn

154. Tagalong - Mahal Kita / Iniibig kita

155. Tahitian - Ua here au ia oe

156. Taiwanese - Wa ga ei li

157. Tamil - Naan Unnai Khadalikkeren

158. Telugu - Nenu Ninnu Premisthunnanu

159. Thailand - Khao Raak Thoe / chun raak ter

160. Tunisian - Ha eh bak

161. Turkish - Seni Seviyorum

162. Ukrainian - Yalleh blutebeh / ya tebe kohayu

163. Urdu - Mea tum se pyaar karta hu (to a girl)

164. Urdu - Mea tum se pyar karti hu (to a boy)

165. Vietnamese (Females) - Em yeu Anh

166. Vietnamese (Males) - Anh yeu Em

167. Vlaams - Ik hue van ye

168. Vulcan - Wani ra yana ro aisha

169. Welsh - Rwy'n dy garu di

170. Wolof - Da ma la nope

171. Yiddish - Ich han dich lib

172. Yoruba - Mo ni fe

173. Yucatec Maya - 'in k'aatech (the love of lovers)

174. Yugoslavian - Ya te volim

175. Zambia (Chibemba) - Nali ku temwa

176. Zazi - Ezhele hezdege (sp?)

177. Zimbabwe - Ndinokuda

178. Zulu - Mina funani wena

I Have a Special Gift for My Readers

I appreciate my readers for without them I am just another struggling author attempting to make ends meet.

My readers and I have in common a passion for the written word as well as the desire to learn and grow from books.

My special offer to you is a massive ebook library that I have compiled over the years. It contains hundreds of fiction and non-fiction ebooks in Adobe Acrobat PDF format as well as the Greek classics and old literary classics too.

In fact, this library is so massive to completely download the entire library will require over 5 GBs open on your desktop.

Use the link below and scan all of the ebooks in the library. You can select the ebooks you want individually or download the entire library.

The link below does not expire after a given time period so you are free to return for more books rather than clog your desktop. And feel free to give the link to your friends who enjoy reading too.

I thank you for reading my book and hope if you are pleased that you will leave me an honest review so that I can improve my work and or write books that appeal to your interests.

Okay, here is the link…

http://tinyurl.com/special-readers-promo

PS: If you wish to reach me personally for any reason you may simply write to mailto:support@epubwealth.com.

I answer all of my emails so rest assured I will respond.

Meet the Author

Dr. Harry Jay is Director of Research for Applied Mind Sciences, a mental health and mind research group, and is the author of over 100 books and research papers spanning his 31-year career as a behavioral scientist. He resides in Southern Utah and enjoys the outdoors, fishing and photography.

http://www.amazon.com/author/harryjay

Visit some of his websites

http://appliedmindsciences.com/
http://appliedwebinfo.com/
http://embarrassingproblemsfix.com/
http://www.epubwealth.com/
http://forensicsnation.com/
http://www.freebiesnation.com/
http://neternatives.com/
http://privacynations.com/
http://refernationwordofmouth.com/
http://survivalnations.com/
http://texternation.com/
http://thebentonkitchen.com
http://theolegions.org
http://willilookgoodinthis.com

Some Other Books You May Enjoy

21st Century Marketing Genius
http://www.amazon.com/dp/B008A07WBW

Addictions
http://www.amazon.com/dp/B006IGHQD4
Anatomy of Anxiety
http://www.amazon.com/dp/B00777QQYS
Applied Income Model
http://www.amazon.com/dp/B006WZN8M4
Applied Mind Sciences
http://www.amazon.com/dp/B007GK4U08
AWeber For Dummies
http://www.amazon.com/dp/B006IVMP8A
A Woman Surrounds A Man
http://www.amazon.com/dp/B008DY2VDO
Be A Prepper
http://www.amazon.com/dp/B007IL5OE6
Be Prepared to Survive
http://www.amazon.com/dp/B007KJ0ANQ
BlueprintCashPro
http://www.amazon.com/dp/B006X0UASS
Blame Me Not
http://www.amazon.com/dp/B008D37AI6
Body Language
http://www.amazon.com/dp/B006INI18G
Body Talk
http://www.amazon.com/dp/B0079MA1XS
Bully America
http://www.amazon.com/dp/B008EJ6102
Cartoon Psychology
http://www.amazon.com/dp/B006IUHMN4
CashCodePro
http://www.amazon.com/dp/B006WZRCVM
Chasing Shadows
http://www.amazon.com/dp/B008A5ZRW8
Chelation Therapy

http://www.amazon.com/dp/B006J7YZ54
Confessions of a Child Predator
http://www.amazon.com/dp/B007BB97KU
Confessions of a Satanic Worshipper
http://www.amazon.com/dp//B007DR4838
Control Your Dreams
http://www.amazon.com/dp/B0071YN3L6
Cyber-Daters Beware
http://www.amazon.com/dp/B006J9T4NA
Distraction Marketing
http://www.amazon.com/dp/B006IUVBWM
Dropping Off The Grid
http://www.amazon.com/dp/B006JLGKLC
Drop Three Dress Sizes in 30-Days
http://www.amazon.com/dp/B007F7VHZI
Effective Email Advertising
http://www.amazon.com/dp/B006IV2300
Embarrassing Problems Fix - General Problems Vol 1
http://www.amazon.com/dp/B0075LOK3U
Embarrassing Problems Fix - Female Problems Vol 2
http://www.amazon.com/dp/B0075LO7AQ
Embarrassing Problems Fix - Male Problems Vol 3
http://www.amazon.com/dp/B0075LQNF8
Energy Psychology
http://www.amazon.com/dp/B006JOZ7G8
Famous Cartoon Quotations
http://www.amazon.com/dp/B007POZKNQ
Famous Quotations
http://www.amazon.com/dp/B007IRKDM8
Female Wolf Packs

http://www.amazon.com/dp/B006JMHD80
ForensicsNation Bushwhacker Program
http://www.amazon.com/dp/B007I9AHVS
ForensicsNationsStore.com Catalog
http://ForensicsNationStore.com
FreebiesNation Blueprint Program
http://www.amazon.com/dp/B007IFRQ9S
Gender Differences in Advertising
http://www.amazon.com/dp/B006IOCG9U
Howdie Doodie
http://www.amazon.com/dp/B00770WQXA
If It Is Broke; Fix It
http://www.amazon.com/dp/B006JM6NHM
I Have a Mind to Believe
http://www.amazon.com/dp/B006ITGY84
I Know I Am But Who Are You
http://www.amazon.com/dp/B006IOQL7I
In-Image Ads Marketing
http://www.amazon.com/dp/B006X03NBE
Interesting Facts About Left-Handed People
http://www.amazon.com/dp/B00744PXCA
Investment Phrases
http://www.amazon.com/dp/B008LO3Y00
It's All About Database
http://www.amazon.com/dp/B006JO0RBI
Latin Phrases
http://www.amazon.com/dp/B006ITY7TW
Legal Phrases
http://www.amazon.com/dp/B008LOA0Q6
Living Alone
http://www.amazon.com/dp/B008601ZC4
Love is the Way
http://www.amazon.com/dp/B006IVYPFG

Male-Female Realities
http://www.amazon.com/dp/B006ITYUNK
Man Up - The Decline and Fall of Manhood
http://www.amazon.com/dp/B006JA2UMG
Massive Traffic Generator
http://www.amazon.com/dp/B006IV1YRS
Men & Women…attract or attack
http://www.amazon.com/dp/B006IU8LU2
Mobile Commerce Blueprint
http://www.amazon.com/dp/B006JO1CX0
Mobile Text Voting
http://www.amazon.com/dp/B006JOI4ZO
Pay Per Call Marketing
http://www.amazon.com/dp/B006XVUD98
Pay Per View Advertising
http://www.amazon.com/dp/B006ZXMI4W
PhattyFat WheytLoss
http://www.amazon.com/dp/B00779O2JW
PLR Cash Tactics
http://www.amazon.com/dp/B006IVGBDU
Questions
http://www.amazon.com/dp/B006WQ715S
Real Estate Phrases
http://www.amazon.com/dp/B008LQ7BMK
Satisfaction
http://www.amazon.com/dp/B006JM6ING
Selling Air
http://www.amazon.com/dp/B006JOIS5K
SEONemo ThenSEO
http://www.amazon.com/dp/B006JN54LW
SEONemo NowSEO
http://www.amazon.com/dp/B006JMYHYI
SEONemo SoonSEO

http://www.amazon.com/dp/B006JN5606
SMS Mobile Competitions
http://www.amazon.com/dp/B006JO1MLC
SMS Reverse Auction
http://www.amazon.com/dp/B006JOYKI4
Social Media Marketing
http://www.amazon.com/dp/B006Z7VSGW
Stealing You
http://www.amazon.com/dp/B00778TT6E
Surviving A Financial Crisis
http://www.amazon.com/dp/B007J1QH3C
Surviving YOU
http://www.amazon.com/dp/B007J3M6A8
Teen Idols
http://www.amazon.com/dp/B006IWNPYC
The Color of White
http://www.amazon.com/dp/B008GNIOTM
The Complete Health System
http://www.amazon.com/dp/B006IVHG2K
The Denial of Self
http://www.amazon.com/dp/B008B7OK32
The ePubWealth Program
http://www.amazon.com/dp/B008HHHVO6
The Face of Anorexia
http://www.amazon.com/dp/B007F8M4XG
The Face Of Despair
http://www.amazon.com/dp/B006JPOV2S
The Greatest Fraud the World Has Ever Known
http://www.amazon.com/dp/B008GUBKI2
The Missing Link
http://www.amazon.com/dp/B006WQLNTI
The Other Side of Me
http://www.amazon.com/dp/B006JMYAE0

The Pain Game
http://www.amazon.com/dp/B007DIPZX4
The Postcarders
http://www.amazon.com/dp/B006IUUV6O
The Power of Observation
http://www.amazon.com/dp/B006IU99EY
The Psychology of Sales
http://www.amazon.com/dp/B006IUH0GI
The Science of Psychology EXPOSED
http://www.amazon.com/dp/B007JBR682
The Smack Report
http://www.amazon.com/dp/B007AZIELK
The Story of Stupid
http://www.amazon.com/dp/B007L2QCHK
The Truth About Federal Anti-Hoarding Laws
http://www.amazon.com/dp/B007J4KH4O
The Truth About Snow Skiing
http://www.amazon.com/dp/B0072R1SAU
The Vowel Movement
http://www.amazon.com/dp/B0071NUPZY
To Boldly Go Mobile
http://www.amazon.com/dp/B006JNJTEK
Too Late For Fruit; Too Soon For Flowers
http://www.amazon.com/dp/B006IVLXSI
Traffic Jam
http://www.amazon.com/dp/B007SXI0YK
Traffic Media
http://www.amazon.com/dp/B006IUZV28
Video Marketing
http://www.amazon.com/dp/B006XW0J0U
Web Traffic Systems
http://www.amazon.com/dp/B006IVGYAA
What Is It About Yorkies

http://www.amazon.com/dp/B006JMNRQW
Why Men Should Not Be Allowed To Babysit
http://www.amazon.com/dp/B006JMNR6C
Why Women Should Not Use Online Dating Services
http://www.amazon.com/dp/B006J9EMH8
Will I Look Good In This
http://www.amazon.com/dp/B007NCFZ30
Word of Mouth Marketing (WOMM)
http://www.amazon.com/dp/B006X0FXU8
Wordz
http://www.amazon.com/dp/B006IOCSVQ
You Can Run But You Cannot Hide
http://www.amazon.com/dp/B006JLVZC6
You Can't or You Won't
http://www.amazon.com/dp/B007FQ2EJ2

Novels
Common Ground
http://www.amazon.com/dp/B006I5B1YU
Until The Next Time
http://www.amazon.com/dp/B006I7X5JW
No Crimes Beyond Forgiveness
http://www.amazon.com/dp/B006I7WOSA
The Writing of the Wrong
http://www.amazon.com/dp/B006I9FOPI

Religion
BibleBits
http://www.amazon.com/dp/B006ZD702C
Bible Mysteries
http://www.amazon.com/dp/B007J1WZSI
In The Mind of Christ

http://www.amazon.com/dp/B006ZCC8JS
Pastors as Counselors
http://www.amazon.com/dp/B006ZD0I5S
Small Christians
http://www.amazon.com/dp/B008MX216S
The Covenants of the Bible
http://www.amazon.com/dp/B007J3M2GG
The Names of Angels
http://www.amazon.com/dp/B0084S7W9M
The Ten Commitments
http://www.amazon.com/dp/B007LHTR04
Truthful Christianity, Judaism, and Islam
http://www.amazon.com/dp/B007JMIL2G

Made in the USA
Columbia, SC
04 December 2023